CW00739752

BLACK LEATHER LUCIFER

BLACK LEATHER LUCIFER

ISBN 978-1-902588-27-8

Published 2012 by Glitter Books

Edited and compiled by Jack Hunter

Copyright © Glitter Books 2012

Parts of this book first published in "Moonchild" (2001) by Creation Books, and reprinted with permission

All world rights reserved

CULT MOVIE FILES

INTRODUCTION
FORCE AND FIRE

The work of Kenneth Anger provides a subversive alternative to mainstream cinema that also references this world, and quotes from it. Anger was fascinated by Hollywood history and the escapist glamor of Hollywood movies – especially silent cinema – and mainstream Hollywood functions both as his matrix and his adversary. In his *Hollywood Babylon* books, images of Hollywood stars are taken out of their usual structures of representation and put into a new, perverse context intended to disturb customary modes of perception. These books, like Anger's films, serve to highlight the very ambivalent dynamic between the cinema audience, and the stars they worship and destroy.[1]

For Anger, cinematic projection is an actual ceremony (rather than a re-enactment of something previously staged). It can therefore also function in the form of a prophecy – and, from time to time, a hex. As his films demonstrate, Anger believes strongly in what he describes as the "cinema of correspondences". He regards film as having the potential, when properly used, to invoke primal forces, perhaps even demons. Once released, these demons can affect not only those involved in the film's production, but also, through a series of occult circuits connecting physical with spiritual dimensions of existence, the film's audience. Anger claims that he's always considered movies to be evil; the point of cinematic images, he believes, is to "control" lives and occurrences. "My reason for filming has nothing to do with 'cinema' at all", he claims. "It's a transparent excuse for capturing people… I consider myself as working Evil in an evil medium". He regards film as a kind of terrorist aesthetic, a form of alchemy which works to bring both image and spectacle to life. Anger's *Hollywood Babylon* books, in fact, are chronicles of the ways in which lives have been cursed and destroyed by the demons of film.

"Lucifer", writes Kenneth Anger, "is the patron saint of the visual arts. Color, form, all these are the work of Lucifer". It was Anger who first understood that film, properly used and respected, is a spiritual form, a magical ceremony involving the display of trapped light. We often forget that the word "media" is the plural of the word "medium", the most common word for a channeler of spirits. The filmmaker is an artist working in light, his camera a ceremonial instrument of invocation, the cinematograph his magical sceptre. And the lord of light, of course, is Lucifer.

Anger's first screen appearance, according to the filmmaker himself, took place in 1935, when he played the part of the Changeling Prince in the MGM Max Reinhardt-William Dieterle version of *A Midsummer Night's Dream*.[2] However, since Anger's name does not appear in the cast or credit listings, there is – typically – doubt whether or not he actually appeared in the film. In stills from the movie, the Changeling Prince does appear very much like Kenneth Anger might have looked as a child; however, those familiar with Anger's propensity for self-mythography have suggested that the role was actually played not by Anger, but by a little girl. That such doubt exists, is testament to the brilliance with which Anger has interwoven strands of fact and meta-fiction to present his own life as a work of art in itself, in which his movies themselves reside as contained and concentrated eruptions of "evil" energy, landmarks on the artist's voyage to illumination.

When Anger first began making his films in the 1940s, he designed his work to cast a spell over its audience by means of a creative synthesis of all aspects of the filmmaking process – cinematography, lighting, set design, wardrobe, acting, editing, lab printing, and projection. The intention behind films like *Puce Moment* (1949) and *Inauguration Of The Pleasure Dome* (1954) was to open up the cinematic experience to new levels of consciousness not ordinarily attained during "normal' daily life. The esoteric nature of these films is designed to help the audience attain an altered state of mind. Indeed, Anger once said that he wished he could bypass film completely and project images directly into the viewer's mind.

In later films like *Scorpio Rising* (1963), *Lucifer Rising* (1966) and *Invocation Of My Demon Brother* (1969), Anger experimented with montage editing, projected, superimposed images and other forms of cineplastics in an attempt to realize more fully the esoteric magic of the cinematic process. For Anger, a screening of one of his films was a serious, potentially dangerous alchemical ritual, a kind of technical, hypnotic form of astral projection. The sinister, hermetic symbolism of *Lucifer Rising*, like the arcane optical effects of *Invocation Of My Demon Brother*, are brilliant shadows cast by the perverse imagination of a master magician. To Anger, himself a high-level practitioner of occult magic (and disciple of Aleister Crowley), making movies was a way of casting spells in the form of "shadow prints". By combining the regular and the structured with images of chaos (such as having the whole screen shimmer with glitter), Anger attempts to induce a state of hypnosis in the viewer, which will then leave them more receptive to occult signs and symbols. He also experiments with techniques like multiple exposures, subliminal cuts, celluloid that is scratched to create a glittering spray, abrasive editing, documentary elements and the use of strobes, split screens and hypnotic waves of sound.

Lucifer Rising, to touch on just one example of Anger's cinematic style, is intended to function like a spell, invoking feelings of anxiety and trauma in the film's audience through a free-form exercise in dream imagery involving taboo realms, mainly homoeroticism. Imaginative, hypnotic presentations of violence and perversion use the rich texture of myth to explore psychological conditions, focusing mainly on sexual neurosis. The montage of hermetic symbols becomes first dreamlike, then menacing; centuries of mystical thought are distilled into a series of voyeuristic fantasies, a kinky psychodrama backed by the carnival strains of a malefic calliope. Anger intended *Lucifer Rising* to stand as a form of ritual marking the death of old religions like Judaism and Christianity, and the ascension of the more nihilistic Age of Lucifer. The old era burns itself out as the new one is born. To symbolize this process, occult images are mapped onto images taken from contemporary popular and youth cultures to create a series of ironic montages, an alchemical transformation achieved through the invocation of cinematic demons.

To point out that cinema has a transcendent potential isn't to stray too far from most people's realm of experience. Who hasn't been mesmerized, horrified, sexually aroused or moved to tears by the power of film? It seems to be a fairly widely held assumption that film has the power to provoke lust, inspire crimes and cause madness, as well as to bless, and perhaps even to heal. Like all forms of art, cinema is a spiritual medium full of sublime metaphysical possibilities, with the capacity to provoke all kinds of intense and profound emotions, perceptions, insights and prophecies: the truths of trapped light.

Sadly, however, few filmmakers other than Anger have been brave enough to acknowledge the rapturous, elemental possibilities of cinema for taking us beyond what is "real" and "natural" to the sacred, hermetic realm of mechanism and artifice. In an essay called "Modesty And The Art Of Film" published in *Cahiers Du Cinéma* in 1951, Anger describes the neglected art of this kind of abstract, non-realist cinema as the "reflection of the divine fire of inspiration":

"[T]his transient fire, this flash of light which appears out of the night and has to be given expression and yet which sometimes has the incandescent force of a newly-born volcano – is a fragile thing: a witch's light, St. Elmo's fire. What Eisenstein called 'the first vision'. What a strange paradox, then, is the film medium, that magnificent and terrible instrument born of our time to tempt and torture our creative imagination..."

Anger's 1951 essay is actually a very eloquently voiced complaint about Hollywood's obsession with "the grandiose, the epic, the big" – that is, the commercially profitable, rather than the smaller scale, the more lyrical, poetic and personal. Anger argues that large-scale films necessitate a rigid commercial control that sacrifices freedom and spontaneity for the sake of a highly refined style and formulaic narrative. And if this were the case in 1951, how much more the case it is today, when it's virtually impossible to find a venue for films that are anything less than feature length, or in any way experimental in their formal and technical properties.

Anger concludes his article in *Cahiers Du Cinéma* with a call to those prophets of "personal lyricism" who have the courage to "restore faith in a pure cinema of sensual revelation", to "re-establish the primacy of the image", to "teach us the principles of their faith: that we participate before evaluating". With the help of such prophets, claims Anger, "[w]e will give back to the dream its first state of veneration" and "recall primitive mysteries":

"The future of film is in the hands of the poet and his camera. Hidden away are the followers of a faith in 'pure cinema', even in this unlikely age. They make their modest 'fireworks' in secret, showing them from time to time; they pass unnoticed in the glare of the 'silver rain' of the commercial cinema. Maybe one of these sparks will liberate the cinema...."

NOTES

1. Originally deemed unprintable in English for fear of libel suits, *Hollywood Babylon* was first published in Paris, 1959, by Jean-Jacques Pauvert. The first English edition was published in the USA by Straight Arrow Books, in 1975 – although a semi-official version had been published in 1964 by notorious literary bootlegger Marvin Miller (who also produced a shoddy softcore porn movie version in 1971).

In his introduction, Anger outlines his primary concept, aligning the pantheon of Golden Age Hollywood stars with much more ancient deities and archetypes, and foreboding the resultant implications of tragedy, madness and death.

"...There was Venus and Adonis only called Clara and Rudy; there was Pan called Charlie; there was even old Bacchus named Fatty and maimed Vulcan named Lon. It was an illusion, a tease, a fraud; it was almost as much fun as the 'old-time religion' without blood on the altars. But the blood would come..."

2. With its fairy-tale/magical imagery recalling the films of Jean Cocteau – in some ways Anger's cinematic mentor – *A Midsummer Night's Dream* is the ideal debut vehicle for a future celluloid magus. Whether or not Anger played the Changeling, the film remains an interesting pointer toward many of his future cinematic concerns. Nikolas Schreck, in his seminal account of occult/diabolic cinema *The Satanic Screen*: "(Anger's) fascination with the mysteries of the movies began as a child, when he had a bit part in *A Midsummer Night's Dream* (1935) directed by Max Reinhardt and William Dieterle. Other important figures in the Satanic cinema, such as Paul Wegener, Edgar Ulmer and Hans Poelzig had worked under Reinhardt's direction. Dieterle, who co-directed Anger's first appearance in film, had appeared in Murnau's *Faust* and later directed *The Devil And Daniel Webster*. It's instructive to view Anger's own magical films as forming part of a continuum with these earlier evocations of Lucifer. The role young Anger played in the picture, that of a changeling, has always been connected with the darker side of the faery domain. He described the experience as a 'rite of passage', and 'the shining moment of my childhood'." (p80).

MYTH AND SYMBOLISM
BLUE VELVET

"I've always considered movies evil; the day that cinema was invented was a black day for mankind."
–Kenneth Anger

The cinema of Kenneth Anger represents a type of film Symbolism that is uniquely analogous to the theory of correspondences basic to the Symbolist tradition. Here, as J.E. Cirlot has written:

"...all cosmic phenomena are limited and serial and... they appear as scales or series on separate planes... the components of one series are linked with those of another in their essence and in their ultimate significance... There is also a psychological basis for the theory of correspondences related to synaesthesia."[1]

Anger's techniques, his experiments with film form, can be compared to certain synaesthetic experiments which were developed by Symbolist poets such as Charles Baudelaire or Arthur Rimbaud.

The films of Kenneth Anger lend themselves well to analysis because he is one of the most exacting craftsmen of the American avant-garde. His refinements in production quality enable him to perform cinematic arabesques of delicacy and complexity which often surpass the conventional cinema's far more expensive "special effects". In fact, Anger demands such technical perfection in his films that he has often been unable to complete his projects and they remain in the form of sketches or fragments. Anger's perfectionism, his attention to detail in all aspects of film production, encourages us to consider him as a film "artisan". (He even restores his own prints by hand, travelling to archives in Europe as well as throughout America in order to preserve his work.) Jack Smith's techniques of "sloppiness" (mouldiness, trash-art, anti-art) are totally excluded from Anger's aesthetic[2]. Anger believes in the application of skill. His is a vision which, like Gustave Moreau's, has been achieved through the patient application of technique, and, like Moreau, he is sometimes over-ambitious. The most famous of Moreau's paintings, *Les Chimères*, was one which he never finished, although he reworked the figures of this canvas longer than those in any of his other works.

Many analogies can be drawn between the Baudelaire-inspired school of French Decadence/Symbolism and the world view expressed in the films of Jack Smith and Andy Warhol. These "Baudelaireans" of the American 1960s visualized images from Decadent themes; or rather, Smith visualized Decadence and Warhol allowed it to expose itself. Anger's Decadent vision is atypical in that he is critical of the Decadent world view; he both expresses and manipulates it. In this way, he is more overtly critical of American society than the other Baudelairean filmmakers. Anger can be understood as a social diarist concerned with the images of the ongoing cultural revolution within the American 1960s, documenting cults, cult-figures, and personalities such as the Hell's Angels, Bobby Beausoleil, Mick Jagger, Marianne Faithfull, et al. Unlike Warhol (who often used identical material), Anger chooses to comment on this material. Yet his themes are derived from a myriad of different myths, cults and social phenomena as well. Anger's content can be understood as Decadent mainly in the context of his images, which are icons taken from a sick and dying society (*Invocation Of My Demon Brother*, *Kustom Kar Kommandos*, *Scorpio Rising*). The images in *Scorpio* or *Invocation* are carefully portrayed as symbolic representations of death. In *Scorpio* objects (tools, machines) are portrayed as fetishes which act as milestones on the protagonist's one-way trip down death's highway. But these images of heroes and objects are presented to us for our judgement, not solely for our titillation. In these films heroes and objects have been carefully selected for their negative as well as seductive qualities. Anger records history as well as demythifies it.

His body of films is particularly suitable for analysis in a Symbolist context because of Anger's own assiduously applied system of "Magick" – a form of Symbolism in which his development of a cinema of correspondences is based on the associative tables of Aleister Crowley. Anger's experiments with the technique of parallel montage form a complementary system of correspondences to "Magick". Elaborately balanced networks of parallel montage operate within these films. We will also examine the ways in which Anger expresses his understanding and application of Sergei Eisenstein's structural principles of montage. The Symbolist system at work in Anger's montage is a realization of what Eisenstein had defined as a form of synaesthesia in the chapters "Synchronisation Of The Senses" and "Colour And Meaning" in his book *The Film Sense*. As is well known, Eisenstein's interest in Symbolism was of tremendous influence in his later work. Peter Wollen has remarked that: "...the dominant strand throughout the rest of his [Eisenstein's] life was to be the investigation of 'the synchronisation of the senses', a return to the symbolist infatuation with Baudelaire's correspondences."[3] It might be said that the Symbolist influences of Aleister Crowley and Sergei Eisenstein, as combined in the works of Kenneth Anger, lead us back to Baudelaire. Georges Sadoul wrote of Maya Deren and Kenneth Anger as the two most important names in the development of the New American Cinema.[4] Both were forerunners of a generation of visionary filmmakers (Brakhage, Harrington, Markopoulos) who began their work in the mid-1940s. Recent critical attempts to draw parallels between the films of Deren and Anger through their mutual preoccupation with mystical ritual are misleading, however. Deren's interest in the occult as a system for depicting an interior state moved away from surrealist psycho-drama and toward a fascination with combining the elements of a given ritual in order to structure her narrative material. Influenced by classical aesthetics, she experimented with transtemporal continuities and discontinuities found in the cinematic structure. With Deren the narrative form orders the subconscious into a design; ritual is used to impose an ideal order on the arbitrary order of art and the chaotic order of the world. The interior event is presented as a matrix out of which a pattern is made, and this pattern of ritual elements is combined to form the overall structure. Historically, it is useful to view Deren as a forerunner of the works of Alain Resnais or modern-day experimental structuralists such as Hollis Frampton, Joyce Weiland, or Michael Snow, rather than to see her work as simply a part of the 'trance film' trend in the early American Underground.

Anger's use of ritual is quite different from any of the above filmmakers. His narrative model is constructed through a comparative analysis of myths, religions, and rituals and their associations external to their respective systems. His two works which give greatest evidence of this are *Inauguration Of The Pleasure Dome* (1954–66) and *Scorpio Rising* (1964).

Deren was concerned with occultism as a classicist, interested in recombining its ritual orders within a system. Anger, a romanticist, sees occultism as a source of hermetic knowledge. For Anger, making a movie is casting a spell. He claims "Magick" as his life-work and the "cinematograph" for his magical weapon.[5] He dubs the collection of his works *The Magick Lantern Cycle*, has adopted Aleister Crowley as his guru[6], sees his films to be a search for light and enlightenment, and sees Lucifer not as the devil but as Venus – the Morning Star.[7] To date, all of his films have been evocations or invocations, attempting to conjure primal forces which, once visually released, are designed to have the effect of "casting a spell" on the audience. The Magick in the film is related to the Magickal effect of the film on the audience.

As a prestidigitator Anger somewhat parallels Georges Méliès: a magician making transformations as well as reconstructions of reality.[8] As a Symbolist operating within the idealist tradition he has a *fin-de-siècle* fascination with ideal artificiality: in *Lucifer Rising* he causes certain landscapes to reveal themselves at their most magical by both capturing the moment and capitalizing on it, showing a rare moment of nature, albeit enhanced through technical effects (such as the hand-tinting and the spellbinding "star machine" which was built at the Chicago Art Institute to play red and green pentagrams over the screen and audience at his most recent presentation of *Lucifer*). Not a surrealist who puts blind faith in his own dream images and trusts his dreams to convey an uncommon unconscious, Anger works pre-dominantly in archetypal symbols. As the magus, he is the juggler of these symbols, just as in the Tarot, where the Magician is represented by the Juggler and is given the attribution of

Mercury, the messenger.

As a visionary, Anger creates his own frame of reference which is an extension of the vision and teachings of Aleister Crowley. Crowley has been called the "Oscar Wilde of Magic", and has called himself "The Beast 666". The English magus born in 1875, he was a contemporary and enemy of both Freud and Yeats. He quarrelled with the latter over leadership in the Hermetic Order of The Golden Dawn. Although he claimed, in criticizing Freud, "I cannot do evil that good may come. I abhor Jesuitry. I would rather lose than win by stratagem"[9], he is reputed to have jumped official rank in The Order, illegitimately claiming the title of Ipsissimus:

"There was yet another order within the Great White Brotherhood, the top order; it bore the name of the Silver Star... (Astrum Argentinium). This contained the three exalted grades – Master of the Temple, Magus, and Ipsissimus... they were on the other side of the Abyss."[10]

Entering into this ultimate enlightenment as Master of the Temple and exiting as self-ordained god, Crowley and his discovery of supreme apotheosis of the self produced his "do as thou wilt" philosophy. In his *Book Of The Law* (the means by which he bridged the Abyss to Masterhood) he proclaimed: "Bind Nothing. Let there be no difference made between any one thing and another... The word of Sin is Restriction... there is no law beyond 'Do What Thou Wilt'."[11] Crowley's self-deification is reflected in the "joyful humanism" of the Age of Horus or the Aquarian Age. The Cosmology of his

Book Of The Law introduces this third Aeon: after Isis' aeon of matriarchy and Osiris' aeon of patriarchy follows the aeon of Horus, the Child or true self independent of priests or gods. In his *777 – Book Of Correspondences*, Crowley cross-indexes Greek, Egyptian, and Hindu mythologies. Venus is found in Isis and corresponding goddesses. Lucifer is the Roman name for the planet Venus which was worshipped both as Aurora (the morning star) and Vesper (the evening star). Until these myths were suppressed by the Catholic Church the Gnostics worshipped Aurora/Lucifer as the Herald of the Dawn, the light preceding the sun. The Crowleyan/Anger doctrine exchanges Lucifer with Horus as well:

"It all began with a child playing with a chemistry set that exploded," Anger has explained, "an innocent, pure child prodigy, creating for the joy of it, just as Lucifer created his own light shows in heaven... Eventually he was expelled for playing the stereo too loud."[12]

Like Cervantes' *mas bello que Dios*, Lucifer's sins lie in outdoing God. He is seen not as a leader but as the totally independent, original rebel: the Luciferean spirit manifests itself in the spirit of the artist, not as a Hell's Angel. "He is also Puck [the name of Anger's production company], the spirit of mischief, mortals are the toys in his playpen, the world belongs to Lucifer."[13]

But Crowley's major contribution to Anger's vision was his invention of "Magick", the performance of ritual which seeks to invoke the Holy Guardian Angel (the aspirant's higher self), an idea adapted from the medieval magus Abra-Melin.[14] The method of invocation relies on talismanic magic: the vitalization of talismans. Originally these were drawn vellum patterns, sort of a shadowgraph print of the demon one sought to "capture".

Anger equates this with the photograph's ability to steal the soul of the subject. Medieval talismanic signatures were considered to be autographs by demons and Anger refers to them as printed circuits between physical and spiritual (or alternative) reality. He sees glyphs, hieroglyphs, sigils, pictographs, billboards, and especially tattoos as magickal marks on the wall.[15] In *Lucifer* he uses the Abra-Melin "Keys" or trademarks of the basic elements as overlaid inscriptions which interact with the visual energies of earth, air, fire, and water so that the symbols "call forth" variations in their visual counterparts. "Magickal" insignias are an integral system at work in all of Anger's films. They are duly consecrated by optical isolation through special effects: the triangular "trademark" matted into a shot of Isis in *Lucifer*, the mirrored superimposition of magickal tattoos on Anger's arms in *Invocation Of My Demon Brother* (1969), a door within Crowley's face which opens into a superimposed zodiac in *Inauguration Of The Pleasure Dome*, the hand-tinted chartreuse fan ("the magickal weapon") in the otherwise blue-toned *Eaux d'Artifice* (1953) and, most recently, the addition of hand-tinting in *Lucifer* which unites the flying falcon-of-Horus and the live Kephra scarab with their carved hieroglyphs.

To conjure a successful transformation Anger-as-Magus-Artist mixes his palette according to Crowley's colour system from the Golden Dawn (a Rosicrucian order): a codified alchemical scale wherein planets are related to colours, sacred alphabets, drugs, perfumes, jewels, plants, magical weapons, the elements, the Tarot, etc, etc. In the Royal Colour Tables of *777 – The Book Of Correspondences* the "princess Scale" denotes the pure, pastel colours of idealism.[16] This is the scale which Anger applies to his brief-but-beautiful *Kustom Kar Kommandos* (1965). In *KKK* he makes his invocation through the use of colour, attempting the transposition of the sign of Cancer (seashell blue and pink) onto the Machine. The pastels of reflected flesh and the hard gleam of the dream buggy, from the knight on the hood to the tyres, are edited together to resemble the languid movements of a boa constrictor. Dedicated to the Charioteer of the Tarot, the "dream lover" owner of the car, is Anger's "silver knight in shining armour".[17] Like the car, he is a machine built for transmitting energy; the blond boy is seated in a mirrored chamber with velvet seats designed to resemble a vulva or giant twin lips, forming a red plush vertical smile. Anger feels that *KKK* closely resembles Salvador Dalí's painting *Mae West's Living Room* in the portrayal of a maternal universe wherein power is a poetic extension of personality, an accessible means of wish-fulfilment. The lyrics "I want a dream lover so I don't have to dream alone..."[18] enrich the romanticism within the phallo-centric vision of narcissistic-identification-as-virility. A dream lover is a double, a "demon brother" and a mirror-reflection; *KKK* is an invocation of the ideal, not human elements, and is dedicated to an idealization of reality.

Romantic idealization, poetic irony, lush exoticism, and the evolution of anti-classicist montage wherein the whole is subordinate to the parts all reflect Anger's affinity with *fin-de-siècle* French literature. (In 1951 he attempted to film Lautréamont's *Les Chants de Maldoror* [1868]). His most profuse use of Decadent/Symbolist imagery occurs in *Inauguration Of The Pleasure Dome*. However, the development of a montage-syntax that closely resembles the elaborate syntactical constructions of Joris-Karl Huysmans and the ambiguities of Ducassian mixed metaphor[19] are nowhere more evident than in *Scorpio Rising*.

Scorpio Rising is an extension of self-gratification into self-immolation. The Machine (now a motorcycle) is totemized into a tool for power: the "charioteer" is Death (the ultimate "dream lover" by romantic standards). Violence replaces the poetic extension of personality and violent eroticism is combined with the tragic death of the highway hero ("the last cowboys"): "*Scorpio Rising* is a machine and Kenneth Anger keeps his spark plug burning on AC [Aleister Crowley] current... Guess which one I was in love with ten years ago?... Was it the chromium or was it the guy?"[20]

Sado-masochism, death and sensuality, sex and angst – *Scorpio* is America's buried collective adolescence manifested in the isolated pop-art visions of decayed dreams. It reflects

the last gasp of the dying Age of Pisces (Christianity) as a motorcycle race roaring toward oblivion. The big butch bikers encase themselves in leather: slung with chains they move indolently, like huge cats. Scorpio and his brothers/lovers ("Taurus" and "Leo" – both ruled by Venus) worship their machines. But people as well as objects denote fetishism, are transformed through mass adulation into becoming idols. James Dean is shown as the Aquarian Rebel Son; Brando, Christ, Hitler – all are objects of worship, humans idolized by idiots... The different degree of impact each had was dependent on the degree of advertising between pop stars and Christ.[21] A grade-C Christ film, *The Road To Jerusalem*, produced by Family Films, was delivered to Anger's doorstep by mistake while he was in the process of editing *Scorpio Rising*; he accepted it as a gift from the gods, toned it blue and intercut it (as the second major montage element within the film) with the bikers' Halloween party. Christ is introduced walking with his disciples on Palm Sunday, two of the "theme songs" ("I Will Follow Him" and "He's A Rebel") link the Christ scenes to Brando and Dean; "Torture" (Gene McDaniels) and "Wipeout" (The Surfaris) link Him to the bikers' initiation and Hitler. The purpose of "following Him" is to race after the trophy, dying to be first, just as the sperm is racing toward oblivion in its desperate need to unite with the egg. The "egg" may well be the new aeon and the longed-for oblivion: the destruction necessitated by change. The new aeon is reached by moving from Scorpio's "night" toward Lucifer's "dawn". The skull-and-crossbones fluttering in super-imposition over the cycle rally signifies the death of sensuality in much the same way as the death's head on the Masonic or Rosicrucian flags represents the philosophical death of man's sensuous personality – a transition considered essential in the process of liberating man's spiritual nature. The final shot of the film is the dead Scorpio's outstretched arm, lit by the red strobe of a patrol car, on it the tattoo "Blessed, Blessed Oblivion".

Anger's myths address mass erotic-consciousness through a barrage of notorious symbols. These often war with one another in Reichian power-trips of rape, will power, fascism, and revolution. "I find ridiculous the idea of anyone being the leader", Anger has said.[22] Pentagrams war with swastikas in *Invocation Of My Demon Brother*. Brando tortures Christ in *Scorpio*; Shiva asserts absolute power over his guests in *Pleasure Dome*. Historical heroes are reduced to pop-idols and history is demythified by comic book codes (When earths collide, gods die).

Considering that Anger takes an anti-nostalgia stance and deplores the fact that yesterday's heroes are still with us (Brando), it is ironic that at the time *Scorpio* was released it enjoyed popularity as a dirty Halloween party or as a celebration of the contemporary decadence it displayed. But today the pop *Liebestod* lyrics of the 'sixties ("He's a rebel and he'll never be free...", or "I still can see blue velvet through my tears") have strong nostalgic resonances. Revived in the

vacuous 'seventies, these lyrics had audiences stomping and clapping to the very songs which originally served as a criticism of idolatry and romanticism turned in on itself and beginning to rot. The value of Anger's strategic use of pop songs transcends their being structural units within a collage film; they often act as a complicated running commentary in lyric form, performing a narrative as well as structural function. In *Rabbit's Moon*, *Puce Moment*, and *Kustom Kar Kommandos* the result is that the naïve poetry of the song

replaces the temporality of spoken dialogue in a timeless, mythic way. In *Rabbit's Moon* the lyrics "There's a moon out tonight" and "I only have eyes for you" underscore the futility of "reaching for the moon" – a message visually expressed in the repetition of shots of a *commedia*-style Pierrot supplicating a Méliès-style moon which remains just out of reach. *Puce Moment* takes on a spicier meaning when the songs "I'm A Hermit" and "Leaving My Old Life Behind" on the sound-track are combined with the visuals of shimmering antique dresses and a languishing Hollywood star. The obvious suggestion here is a renunciation of drag-dressing, an escape from the fetishization of costume and a climb "out of the closet". Anger's most complex and intriguing use of music occurs in *Eaux d''Artifice,* where light, colour, movement, and textures are combined in baroque counterpoint with Vivaldi. With *Invocation* and *Lucifer* he began to move toward an exclusive use of original musical scores.

Transubstantiation is one of Anger's favourite themes. Frequently this takes the form of a reverse Eucharist where essence is converted into substance; this process can be discovered in *Fireworks* (1947 – his first major film), *Puce Moment*, *Rabbit's Moon*, *Scorpio*, and *Lucifer*. These films summon personifications of forces and spirits whose dynamic powers appear to "break through" and turn against the character and/or structure. *Scorpio*'s iconoclasm is effected by the critique which the film conducts on itself, demythifying the very myths it propounds by interchanging them with one another and integrating them into a metamyth. Christ/Satan (religion), Brando/Dean (popular culture), and Hitler (political history) are reduced to sets of systems which destroy one another through an internarrative "montage-of-attraction".[23] Thus, the film itself is the metamyth of the films which constitute it. Different dogmas are equalized (and subsumed by) their structural and ideological parallels. Scorpio's auto-destruction stems from the centre, "core" invocation and

triumph of Satan over Christ, Machine over Man, Death over Life.

A somewhat less nihilistic subsumation of substance by essence is the conventional Eucharist ritual performed in *Inauguration Of The Pleasure Dome* and *Eaux d'Artifice*. In the former, Lord Shiva transforms his guests into spirits of pure energy which he absorbs and recycles into a frenzied, operatic orgy. The pyrotechnics of this celebration build to such visual intensity that *Pleasure Dome* "destroys" itself by growing too large for the very confines of the screen. In the original (pre-"Sacred Mushroom Edition" – 1958) the screen grew "wings" (like Abel Gance's *Triptych*) and, for the final twenty minutes, each panel of the triptych was loaded with up to six simultaneous surfaces of super-imposition (eighteen separate planes). The visual material seeks to transform itself into pure energy. In *Eaux d'Artifice* "The Lady enters the 'nitetime labyrinth of cascades, balustrades, grottoes, and fountains', and tries to lure out the monsters with her fan; she's trying to invoke the water gods... She fails, being weak and frivolous, and melts into the water (surrenders her identity) so that she can play on."[24] *Eaux* turns its hermaphrodite hero(ine) into a waterfall. Nature wins over artifice. Human confusion is subsumed by the larger order of things.

After thoroughly examining the myths, themes and techniques in Anger's work, we are prepared to examine, in detail, his experiments with montage. Because the most advanced and complex editing techniques appear in *Scorpio*

Rising, it will serve as a model.

We have seen how *Scorpio Rising* portrays the fall of an age, demonstrates a revolution in culture. The catalysts for this change are black-leathered motorcyclists who exist outside and in defiance of the prevailing culture. This self-imposed, romantic alienation and violent defiance give the cyclists a place in American mythology similar to cowboys and gangsters. Anger plays on these national myths and pits them against the myths and symbols (political, religious, and pop-cultural) of the dying age, to their mutual destruction. To achieve this, Anger utilizes Eisenstein's theories of montage and conflict. The concept of intellectual montage which Eisenstein conceived and with which he experimented, is mastered and forcefully executed by Anger in *Scorpio Rising*. Tony Rayns observes that:

"Anger has an amazing instinctive grasp of all the elements of film-making; his films actively work out much of Eisenstein's theoretical writing about the cinema. For instance, Eisenstein's ideal of 'chromophonic' (colour/sound) montage, described in 'The Film Sense', is startlingly achieved in the 'party lights' sequence [in the 'Walpurgis Party'] in Scorpio Rising, where the Ran-Dells' hard, dense arrangement of the song – for the first time in the movie, cutting in before the end of the preceding song – is matched by a thickening in the terms of reference in the montage, while at the same time lyrics relate explicitly to the film's development of its colour scale... it comes nearer [to Eisenstein's theories]

*than anything in commercial cinema, and produces film-
making as rich in resonance as anything of Eisenstein's
own.*"[25]

    Scorpio has the form of a ritual from its beginning, in
preparation, to its end, in death. The cyclic nature of the ritual
suggests a timeless repetition. The film has been divided into
four parts for the ritual. The "boys" meticulously preen their
mechanical egos (cycles), in custom colours and high gloss
chrome, and themselves, in bulging denim and leather. In
"Image Maker" (Part II), Scorpio, the film's hero is
introduced. Through him, Anger probes the contents of the
myth of motorcyclists. The interactions of the image and the
person, each being a manifestation of the other, are explored
through the character Scorpio by contrast with other cultural
heroes (James Dean, Marlon Brando, Jesus Christ). The end of
the "Image Maker" sequence is marked by Scorpio snorting
cocaine, which also signifies the beginning of the rite which
Scorpio directs. The rhythm of the film begins to grow
orgasmically until the cyclist's death in the end ("Blessed,
Blessed Oblivion"). The "Walpurgis Party" is like a tribal rite
or ceremony, a war dance to build the bikers to the proper
emotional-psychological state for the execution of the ritual.
The antics of the bikers at the Walpurgis Party are very erotic,
in a very adolescent way. Scorpio leaves the party to inspect
and desecrate a church. From the church (at night) Scorpio's
demonic possession grows until he is in control of the parallel
action which he directs from the altar. The montage and the

action grow more and more frantic as Scorpio "oversees" the motorcycle race (day), the objective of which is not victory but death (completion of the ritual). It is the death of the cyclist which ends the rite and the film. Eisenstein wrote that "It is art's task to make manifest the contradictions of Being. To form equitable views by stirring up contradictions within the spectator's mind, and to forge accurate intellectual concepts from the dynamic clash of opposing passions."[26]

The importance of Anger's use of Eisensteinian principle is that it is not reduced to a craft, a trick in time, but maintained as an artistic vision. In montage reality is smashed. Art comes from the filmmaker's reassembling of the splinters of time and space with the inclusion of the intellectual, psychological, or emotional content of the event. The collision of two separate images creates a third distinct impression to the viewer. Similarly the blending of two dissimilar images into one accumulative essence yields a poetically metaphoric statement on that which is portrayed. This is the artistic importance of Eisenstein's theory. Its potential is rarely realized in film, and even more rarely as true to theory as in Anger's film.

As one begins to break down the elements of montage contained within the film, it is important to remember what Eisenstein said regarding the interaction of montage sequences. "...methods of montage... become montage constructions proper when they enter into relationship of conflict with each other... within a scheme of mutual relations, echoing and conflicting with one another, they move to a more and more strongly defined type of montage, each one organically growing from the other."[27] When one is examining Anger's use of montage, there are often several levels which must be considered. The montage can seldom be labelled as one specific method without further consideration. For instance, in a montage sequence early in the film, the visual rhythm is created through the song "Wind Up Doll". The song is begun simultaneously with shots of men tightening bolts, or other such action between men and cycles that involves a circular tightening motion. Intercut with these are shots of a young boy playing with a wind-up motor-cycle. Rhythmically the montage sequences are perfectly matched. It is as though the men working on their cycles are winding up the child's toy which is run toward the camera with the child's face in the background. The rhythm established by the song is carried through the montage of the sequences. However, in the conflict of the two images there exists an intellectual montage. The fascination and absorption of the child and man are synonymous. Anger calls it "masculine fascination with the Thing that goes... from toy to terror."[28] The combination of images here gives both a childish innocence and adult ignorance of the consequences of actions to the action of the men. The innocence of the childish fascination is transferred from the child to the men to the extent that the motorcycle seems like a toy. At the same time there is the implication that the power that is building through the winding and tightening will be released for the thrill of movement. The power will be released unhampered by reason, a pure experience, like that of a child.

Anger's use of music for the soundtrack serves a much more vital purpose than merely the creation of rhythm. The thirteen pop tunes which Anger has selected from early 'sixties rock and roll serve not only as a means of organization but also as an ironic narrative. The songs create conflict, on another level, with the images of the film and in this way become an essential part of the film's montage. For example, Anger creates a sexual as well as textural ambiguity through the use of the song "Blue Velvet" combined with montage in which the men dress themselves. The romance of "Blue Velvet" ("She wore blue velvet / And I still can see blue velvet through my tears") on the one hand is in ironic conflict with the very butch masculine men ("she") as they vainly, ceremoniously clothe themselves in tight blue denim ("blue velvet") and black leather with chains. On the other hand, the contents of this sequence are highly eroticized. There are many shots of semi-naked men, muscular chests and stomachs curtained on either side by a black leather jacket. All the eroticism in *Scorpio*, from the adolescent pranks of the Walpurgis Party to the explicit connotations of the sequences now in question, are homo-erotically directed. In one portion of this same sequence a man clothed only in long underwear rises up quickly from the bed into the camera, a full head-on close-up. This shot, in a montage of attractions, is followed by one of a crotch as the man zips up his zipper. The synthesis clearly implies fellatio. Elsewhere, in the Walpurgis Party sequence, this effect is repeated.

Similar to Anger's use of sound to heighten the effect of montage is his use of colour to that same end. The bulk of *Scorpio* was filmed by Anger in colour. Two of the major elements of montage, however, are footage from existing films. The bluish footage of Brando, shot off television, is from the film *The Wild One* (1954). The footage of Christ was also taken from a black and white film which Anger toned blue. Before discussing the significance of colour to montage, let us first examine the sequence in question.

The sequence opens with an ironic intellectual montage which incorporates the misunderstood rebelliousness of adolescence into the character, Scorpio. Scorpio is introduced with the song "Devil In Disguise" ("Looks like an angel but I got wise / You're a devil in disguise"). He is lying on his bed in his room, reading the comics. His walls are cluttered with pictures of motorcycles, James Dean, slogans, etc. The montage forms a relationship between Scorpio, the comics and the things in his room, creating an essence of his personality which is one of the biological fury of adolescence.

At this point, a parallel montage of attraction fuses Brando (the image), who appears on Scorpio's television in the film *The Wild One*, and Scorpio (the person) into one personality. Sitney says of this usage: "It [the television] functions as an aesthetic reactor. Whatever we glimpse on it is

always a metaphor for what is happening within the hero of the film. Its metaphoric level extends simultaneously as an aesthetic dimension of Scorpio's thought and action in the realm of plastic illusion and as an icon of contemporary life – the source as well as the reflection of the unconscious."[29] As Scorpio goes through the action of this sequence, there is a constant interplay between the image qualities of Brando and the reality of Scorpio. Brando smokes, Scorpio smokes: but Scorpio burns his mouth when he tries to light the match on his teeth. When Scorpio dresses (this section is also intercut with footage of men riding motorcycles, real men, not images, filmed in colour, not black and white), as he puts on his leather jacket, Brando turns, revealing the skull on the back of his. Scorpio snorts cocaine, Brando closes his eyes and grins inwardly. But the conflict ends between man and image, the image of Brando leaves the screen, while Scorpio goes out to raise Hell. In fact, the image of Brando is replaced on the screen with a Hebrew menorah and a crucifix, the objects against which Scorpio's violence will be directed.

In the following section of this sequence, Anger creates an overtonal parallel in the montage between Scorpio and Christ. I refer to the montage here as overtonal because while the actions of Christ and Scorpio are parallel in structure, they conflict greatly in motivation; in fact they represent extreme opposites. In this instance the montage is overtonal because of the contradiction inherent in the associations made by the juxtaposition of the shots. The conflict exists between the structure, a parallel montage of attraction (the structure is further aided by the antithetical lyrics of the song "He's A Rebel" which apply equally to Scorpio and Christ), and the content, an overtone to the structure of the section. For example the parallel is introduced as Scorpio leaves his room and walks down the dark street. Christ walks down a street crowded with beggars and cripples. As Christ passes a beggar, there is a cut to Scorpio kicking the grid of his motorcycle. As Christ heals a blind man by touching his eyes, there is a cut to Scorpio touching the throttle of his cycle. As the blind man kneels in gratitude before Christ, there is a four-frame cut to an erect penis that Scorpio would offer him. The parallel is continued through the Walpurgis Party sequence which is contrasted with a gathering of Christ and his disciples. The relationship between the shots are direct, forming a montage of attraction.

The influence of colour on this montage sequence adds yet another dimension. The conflict of colour between the sequences of Christ and Brando (both in bluish-toned black and white) and the bulk of Scorpio (in colour) creates a clear distinction between the mythic qualities of the former and the realism of the latter. Certainly there is an intimate interplay, a give and take between the two, but essentially Anger's goal is to destroy both of these myths. The toning blue of the black and white sequences further adds a sense of romantic longing for the myths and their fading heroes. These are in brutal conflict with the montage of Scorpio and the use of the hard, harsh colour in those sequences. The blue-toned black and white of Brando and Christ coupled with the C-grade production values of *The Road To Jerusalem* also makes those sequences seem artificial. So the colour conflict adds an intellectual slant to the montage of this sequence. Even as the associations are made, one is aware of the artificiality, the invalidity of the Christian and Hollywood myths in contrast to Scorpio and his ritual. The contrast is greatly heightened by the use of colour. Anger has said of this sort of creation "I also

regard the inception of new concepts and viewpoints in the conflict between customary conception and particular representation as dynamic – as a dynamization of the 'traditional view' into a new one."[30]

As we have said before, Eisenstein's principles of montage are an artistic view of reality. We have come to see montage used as a craft, to compress time, or evoke tension. Anger's practice primarily revitalizes the technique of montage and brings in sound and colour in a complementary way. It is interesting that it is a cultural revolution in *Scorpio Rising* which utilizes montage in contrast to Eisenstein's political revolutions in *Battleship Potemkin* (1925) and *October* (1927). Tony Rayns reported that:

"Fascinatingly, Anger plans to use another of Eisenstein's theories in making 'Lucifer Rising'; he wants to explore the possibilities of vertical composition. In his crucial essay 'The Dynamic Square', Eisenstein complains that the advent of cinemascope cripples yet further the adventurous film-maker's chances of breaking away from the limitations of passive horizontal composition: 'It is my purpose to defend the cause of the 50% of compositional possibilities which have been banished from the light of the screen. It is my desire to chant the hymn of the male, the strong, the virile, active, vertical composition! I am not anxious to enter into the dark phallic and sexual ancestry of the vertical shape as a symbol of growth, strength or power...' Naturally enough, this precisely is Anger's desire: 'I guess my whole trip is phallic worship...'."[31]

Before examining the differences in montage technique between *Scorpio Rising* and Anger's later work *Lucifer Rising*, it is necessary to describe its visual content. The title, L-U-C-I-F-E-R R-I-S-I-N-G, rises in vibrating fiery letters from the waves of the ocean. Throughout *Lucifer* neon calligraphy and animated symbols flash, sometimes simultaneously matted onto the landscapes of ancient Egypt. Often these electrified talismans break into the material like signals from lost civilizations: picture-writing erupting through layers of history. *Lucifer*'s universe is populated with signalling gods and alchemical symbols. The work is largely concerned with communication between Isis (Myriam Gibril) and Osiris (Donald Cammell) through the forces of nature; this communion of natural elements provokes meteorological reactions in preparation for Lucifer's arrival: lightning issues forth from the staffs and emblems of these radiant deities; nature replies with rosy dawns, whirlpools, and emissions of molten rock. The sun goes into eclipse. Intercut with an endless torchlight procession, Lilith (Marianne Faithfull) climbs the prehistoric stairway to a Celtic shrine where, as a goddess of the moon, she supplicates the sun. The sun rises directly in the centre of the solstice altar; its rays part to reveal a scarlet demon within the round hole of the rock: the blazing astrological symbol of Mercury (god of communication and ruler of magicians) appears. A magus (Kenneth Anger) stalks around his incandescent magic circle in invocation to the Bringer of Light (cf. Murnau's *Faust*). Outside the smoking circle a Balinese fire demon (symbol of sacrifice) materializes. The magus bows before the idol, a globe of phosphorescent lightning shudders across the screen and Lucifer, resplendent in satin L-U-C-I-F-E-R jockey jacket, arises from within the circle. In response, nature throws a celebration of volcanic eruptions and avalanches of snow and, ultimately, an electrical storm over Stonehenge. Isis and Osiris, the happy parents (of Lucifer-as-Horus) stride through the colonnade at Karnak to greet their offspring, and a feldspar-coloured saucer sails at us from behind the stone head of Ramses II.

So ends the first third of Anger's first, uncompleted, feature, *Lucifer Rising*. This work-in-progress is a remake and continuation of the sabotaged "Love Vision" of Lucifer which he began years ago in San Francisco[32]. The original was to have been about the new tribes of teenagers, turned-on children-teeny-boppers and adolescent hippies, and featured a set of living Tarot tableaux. Today's version of *Lucifer* is as much a departure from its predecessor as it is from the major body of Anger's work. But his previous works can still be understood as pointing the way to this grander, more expansive vision which is less demonic, more divine.

Lucifer Rising attempts to transcend the passive-active dialectics of power and the sexual preoccupations of adolescence, the blue of eternal longing. Its theme (so far) is that of man's reunion with his lost gods: the dawning of a new morality. The cult of arrested adolescence is replaced by the fulfilment of its longing: reaffirmation of identity through spiritual communion between man, gods and nature. Fantasy and reality are no longer distinguished but are parts of a larger, more complete universe. Black Magick goes White; the hero is the "bringer of light", Lucifer, portrayed as a demon of great beauty. This "fire-light-trip" begins with the first frames of *Fireworks* (1947, an invocation to Thor) when a firebrand is extinguished in water[33]. At the film's outrageous finale a sailor's penis is lit and explodes as a roman candle; this is followed by a denouement where a wax candle atop a Christmas tree dips into a fireplace, igniting the scattered stills from the film's opening dream sequence. *Invocation* (resuscitated from the leftover out-takes of the original *Lucifer*, "A fragment made in fury... the last blast of Haight consciousness")[34] opens with an albino demon brother kissing a glass wand; later Mick Jagger's black cat goes up in flames and the film culminates with Bobby Beausoleil short-circuiting into Lucifer. Anger calls *Invocation* a "burn".

There is more light and less fire in *Lucifer Rising* (what the neo-Platonists would refer to as the "spiritual lux"). Assertion of will has matured into communication between anthropomorphic gods; glamorous Egyptian deities within a universe which is established by an uncreated pre-condition for order – pagan spirits at play in a universe where God does not yet exist. These man-gods exist organically, as part of nature; they grow out of the shadow of cliffs and temples like living sculptures. We first see Isis as long legs disembodied by stone shadows. Isis and Osiris, glistening with health and confidence, authentically costumed, perform their nearly static ritual from the cliffs overlooking a space-like sea (Crowley's vast abyss between man and god). Where it was the nature of the stone water gods to overwhelm man in *Eaux*, the "new" gods in Lucifer embody the "best" in man: pure, free forces, calling on nature to aid mankind, summoning the elements in preparation for the Second Coming.

Lucifer is also a radical departure in visual form from Anger's previous works. No longer does the power of any given image depend on the ritualistic repetition and recombination which essentially shapes the overall form of films like *Scorpio* or *Invocation*. *Invocation*'s structure is fumbled and dissonant, an "attack on the sensorium";[35] the entire piece is edited for abrasiveness, any residual flow is destroyed by spasms of electronic shock waves from Jagger's Moog soundtrack. *Scorpio*'s structure works from the inside out: from image to montage to montage-of-attractions to the whole as one entire montage system. The whole is purely a system of inter-relationships and no attempt is made to impose an external order on this network. Image layers mount in density, implications, and velocity toward the climactic "rebel rouser" sequence when Scorpio, performing a black sabbath, transforms himself into his own demon brother and casts his death hex on the cycle rally which, through the montage, seems a swirling continuation of his ceremony of destruction. The use of montage-as-force-field reappears in *Lucifer*'s invocation sequence – the aggressive vitality of tracking camera racing with the sorcerer's movements as he "widdershins" (runs counter-clockwise) around a magic circle. These shots are intercut with an exterior long-shot of baby gorilla and tiger cub chasing around the base of a tree, the movements of nature coinciding with the "unnatural" counter-sun-wise dance of the magus filmmaker. But in this case the sequence is embedded in a less frenetic organization which makes up most of the film.

In *Lucifer* the camera at last liberates its subject matter from its usual medium-close-up iconography through a long-shot/long-take *mise-en-scène*. A series of landscapes, seascapes, skyscapes gain mythical proportions through long-take montage; the long shots establish the vastness of this universe. Lingering takes of the broken pharaoh faces of the Colossus of Memnon have a quality of temporal displacement: they exist outside time and distance as defined by motion of either camera or subject. The impassive statues assume an ancient decadence, exhausted idols compared to the flesh of the living gods. This static vastness which the long-take/long-shot montage creates operates around a vortex or "core" of the film: the invocation sequence which gradually and erratically builds to a spinning force field of compressed energy. This disturbs and changes the natural universe of the film's structure: the exteriors are broken into by collage-inserts, then the external world reasserts itself with long, vertically dynamic takes and vertical wipes: nature rights herself and Lucifer is born.

The piece, as it stands, can be seen either as a complete work in itself or as a chapter with an appropriate ending to a 'forties science-fiction serial. The 1981 version has a film score composed by Bobby Beausoleil, recorded at Tracy Prison[36], and presents a whole vision in itself. With *Lucifer* Anger breaks through his previous nihilism to a "happy ending" (the Crowleyan assertion of love and joy transcending sorrow and sin), dealing with larger, exterior concerns rather than dramas of occult exoticism and decadent ideology. The sun breaks through the clouds.

NOTES

1. J.E. Cirlot, *A Dictionary Of Symbols*, p.60.

2. "The wildest figure of underground film production, who played a central (if unpredictable) role in '60s, '70s and '80s film, was Jack Smith. Born in Columbus, Ohio in 1932, Smith moved to New York in the '50s where he became involved with experimental theatre (studying dance with Ruth St. Denis, and direction with Lee Strasberg) and film (appearing in films by Ken Jacobs such as *Little Cobra Dance: Saturday Afternoon Blood Sacrifice* [1957] and *Blonde Cobra* [1959]). Jack Smith began making his own movies, with the – uncompleted – *Buzzards Over Baghdad* (1951/56), *Overstimulated* (1960), and *Scotch Tape* (1961). Smith's movies were influenced by the glorious-but-tacky Z-grade Arabian Nights and Atlantis movies produced in the '40s and '50s (usually starring Maria Montez), and rich in his own iconography of faded glamour.

In 1963 Smith made his masterpiece, *Flaming Creatures* (Creatures being the people featured in his movies, the term being part of Smith's personal vocabulary), a film which was shot on a bright day on outdated celluloid, resulting in a finished product that appears bleached out (an appearance which is added to by the director's use of muslin and gauze filters). The film itself depicts a Dionysian revelry, shot on the roof of an abandoned building; it pictures various transgressive sexual acts and reaches its climax with a transvestite orgy, cunnilingual rape and simultaneous earthquake. The casual sexuality of the film is emphasized with the exotic attire (drag seems too simple a term) of the protagonists and the erotic flashes of genitals and flesh which serve to confuse the viewer, seducing them into a state in which gender becomes meaningless in the face of a playful sexuality.

When the film was first screened it was seized by the New York Police, and condemned as obscene. Jonas Mekas' (who founded the Filmmakers' Cooperative in 1962) lawyers began defending the film, but the case was dropped, and this resulted in the film being permanently banned in New York.

Smith continued to work in underground film, commencing the unfinished *Normal Love* and producing other fragments subsequently screened under such titles as *Slave President*, *In The Grip Of The Lobster Claw* and *Zombie Of Uncle Pawnshop*. He died in 1989."

–Jack Sargeant, *Deathtripping: The Cinema Of Transgression* (p.7)

3. Peter Wollen, *Signs And Meaning In The Cinema*.

4. Georges Sadoul, *Dictionary Of Film Makers.*

      Maya Deren (1908–61) emigrated to the USA from her native Russia in 1927. In 1943 she made the classic *Meshes Of The Afternoon*, the first part of a trilogy which concluded with *At Land* (1944) and *Ritual In Transfigured Time* (1946). Her other films include *Witches' Cradle* (1944, unfinished), *Meditation On Violence* (1948) and *The Very Eye Of Night* (1959). "Maya Deren always displayed a somnambulistic heroine (played by herself) acting as in a dream or some elaborate ritual, always under the spell of mysterious urges somewhere between desire and great fear, but self-evidently erotic." –Parker Tyler, *Underground Film*

5. Sitney, *Visionary Film.*

6. "I'm engaged in a long-term selling campaign. I have one product that I'm selling: the 20th Century's most misunderstood genius, called Aleister Crowley." –Anger, quoted in Tony Rayns, "Dedication To Create Make Believe".

7. Interview with Anger, Berkeley, California 1974.

8. Georges Méliès (1861–1938) was the pioneer of special effects in early cinema. In many of his 500 films he appeared himself as the Devil, Mephisto, Faust, or an alchemist or magician.

      "...It was the proto-surrealist Méliès who used the cinema to transcend what the Symbolist painter Gustave Moreau dismissed as 'the wretched reporting of positive facts'... Méliès' 1896 *La Manoir Du Diable* is one of the very first presentations of the Devil in the new medium of the cinema... A jumbo-sized bat glides into a *trompe-l'oeil* medieval castle hall set... The bat flaps around menacingly before transforming into a traditionally attired Mephistopheles, none other than Méliès himself. When a cavalier flourishes the despised crucifix, the Devil vanishes in a sulphurous puff of smoke. *Fin.* Essentially, the Devil is portrayed as a stylized grand illusionist, an alter ego of the film-maker."

      –Nikolas Schreck, *The Satanic Screen* (p15)

9. John Symonds & Kenneth Grant, *The Confessions Of Aleister Crowley.*

10. ibid

11. ibid

12. Anger, at a presentation of his films at the San Francisco Art Institute, April 1974.

13. ibid

14. L.W. de Laurence, *The Book Of Sacred Magic Of Abra-Melin, The Mage.*

15. Interview with Anger, Berkeley, California 1974.

16. Aleister Crowley, *777*, p.19.

17. Interview with Anger, Berkeley, California 1974.

18. From the song "Dream Lover", by the Parris Sisters (1959) on Atco

Records.

19. "...faced with strange puns and punctuation; with curious syntactical constructions which weave unexpected opposites into daring new patterns; with grim humour continually dissolving ecstatic lyrical flights in a cloud of ambiguities and teasing commas..."

–Alexis Lykiard, introduction to *Maldoror*.

Isidore Ducasse (1846–70) was born in Montevideo. Little is known of his life. Under the *nom-de-plume* of Le Comte de Lautréamont he published two works: *Les Chants de Maldoror* (1868), and *Poésies* (1869).

Maldoror was particularly adored by André Breton and the Surrealists, and the typical phrase "as beautiful as the chance encounter of a sewing machine and an umbrella on a dissecting table" became a key textual avatar of the Movement.

20. Anger, at a presentation of his films at the San Francisco Art Institute, April 1974.

21. Anger, at a presentation of his films at the San Francisco Art Institute, April 1974.

22. Anger, at a presentation of his films at the San Francisco Art Institute, April 1974.

23. Eisenstein, *Film Sens*e, p.231

24. Tony Rayns, *Anger Kompendium*, p.29.

Russian filmmaker Sergei Eisenstein (1898–1948) found world renown for his early films *Stachka* (*Strike*, 1925) and, in particular, *Bronenosets Potemkin* (*Battleship Potemkin*, 1925), which displayed the director's theories of montage editing and compositional skills to full effect. *Oktiabr* (*October*, 1928) was even more experimental, and poorly received in his native country.

Eisenstein's major later work was *Ivan Groznyi* (*Ivan The Terrible*, 1944–46). When Part 1 of this work was approved by Stalin, Eisenstein stylized Part 2 to his own tastes – as a result, it was not released until 1958, 10 years after his death.

Eisenstein's career was almost as littered with abortive projects as Kenneth Anger's, most notably *Que Viva Mexico!*, a project started after Eisenstein's failure to work in Hollywood in 1930. The intention was to make a film in celebration of Mexico's conflicting cultures of life/death, poverty/wealth, paganism/ Christianity, beauty/corruption, and freedom/oppression. The film went way over-budget, and much of the footage which Eisenstein sent back to America was reportedly pornographic. Fragments of *Que Viva Mexico!* were released variously as *Thunder Over Mexico* (1933), *Time In The Sun* (1939), and *Mexican Symphony* (1942–44) –

all revealing a grotesque black humour conveyed through savage, weird and erotic imagery.

25. Tony Rayns, *Anger Kompendium*, p.26.

      Anger's use of a pop soundtrack is anticipated in Bruce Connor's *Cosmic Ray* (1961), which bases its rapid montage of images around the Ray Charles track "What'd I Say", but Anger takes the concept to a new level in *Scorpio Rising*. This has led to him being labelled the "Godfather of MTV" in some quarters.

      There is little doubt that *Scorpio Rising* was a major influence on later feature films which featured a pop soundtrack, such as Dennis Hopper's *Easy Rider* (1969), Martin Scorsese's *Who's That Knocking On My Door?* (1968) and *Mean Streets* (1973), and George Lucas' *American Graffiti* (1973).

26. Eisenstein, *Film Form* p.46.

27. Eisenstein, *Film Form* p.78–79.

28. Sitney, *Visionary Film*, p.116.

29. Sitney, *Visionary Film*, p.119.

30. Interview with Anger, Berkeley, California 1974.

31. Tony Rayns, *Anger Kompendium*, p.26.

32. "On September 21, 1967, Anger organised a celebration of the Equinox of the Gods at the Straight Theatre on Haight Street. The band played, Anger conducted magick rituals and the proceedings were filmed... Either during or soon after that evening, some 1600 feet of edited rushes for *Lucifer Rising* were stolen, along with some equipment and Anger's car. *Lucife*r had been shot on reversal stock and there was no negative of the missing footage." –Tony Rayns, "Elusive Lucifer"

33. Anger: "Inflammable desires dampened by day under the cold water of consciousness are ignited at night by the libertarian matches of sleep and burst forth in showers of shimmering incandescence..."

34. Interview with Anger, Berkeley, California 1974.

35. Anger, quoted in Tony Rayns, *Anger Kompendium*, p.31.

36. Beausoleil had played Lucifer in the original "missing" version of *Lucifer Rising*. Anger became convinced that Beausoleil was responsible for the theft of the film, and had buried it somewhere in Death Valley. Beausoleil was imprisoned in 1969, charged with the murder of L.A. drug dealer Gary Hinman (see next chapter).

A TORCH FOR LUCIFER

"Making a movie is casting a spell."
–Kenneth Anger

Kenneth Anger's films of the *Magick Lantern Cycle* are an intriguing blend of popular culture, ironic humour and mysticism. As the texts of an occult religious system, they act both as devotional items and potential tools for making new converts. Deliberately aiming to induce an altered state of consciousness in the spectator, they combine extreme subject matter and stunning cinematic innovation. By mixing visual excess with structural discipline, they seek to induce trance.

Focusing on the occult dynamics of the films, after introducing Anger's chosen magickal path, we may consider the operation of his occult aesthetics in particular films and the inability of critical theory to adequately interpret the meaning of Anger's work.

ANGER AND THE OCCULT

Anger is a high-level practitioner of ritual magick. When he performs in his own work, it is invariably in the role of ritualist or Magus. He probably first encountered the writings of English occultist Aleister Crowley in high school[1]. His earliest film in distribution, *Fireworks* (1947) was made when he was 17 in the year of Crowley's death. In 1955, along with Alfred Kinsey, the sexologist, he stayed in Crowley's former Abbey of Thelema in Cefalu, Sicily. Anger worked at restoring Crowley's wall paintings after the whitewashing of Mussolini's regime. He also performed the Magus's rituals in their original setting. "Thelema Abbey", a documentary commissioned by Picture Post's TV *Omnibus* series for British television, was made by Anger at this time, but was lost by the company, so never broadcast. A fictionalised Thelema Abbey, at the "sunset of Crowleyanity" features as the setting of the ritual fantasy *Inauguration Of The Pleasure Dome* (1954).[2]

Crowley, who spelled his magick with a "k" to differentiate it from other kinds, evolved a complex system of ceremonial theory and practice. A former member of the Order of the Golden Dawn, he synthesised an eclectic "Gnostic" system from mythical traditions and modern philosophical and scientific concepts. Crowley's theorems combine originality with deep knowledge of esoteric traditions, including Kabbalism, alchemy, the beliefs of ancient Egypt, Hinduism, Tantra, astrology, and the Arthurian legend. His best-known precepts, "Do What Thou Wilt shall be the Whole of the Law" and "Love is the Law, Love under Will" were given libertarian interpretation in the 1960's. The Beatles included an image of Crowley in their pantheon on the cover of *Sergeant Pepper's*

Lonely Hearts Club Band (1967). During the hippie era, the rigorous spiritual training of the magickian's True Will was disregarded in favour of sexual and narcotic overload.

Crowley's "Every Man and Every Woman is a Star" validates the autonomous power of individual Will[3]. He suggests the magickal potential of every deliberate act. Endorsing a holistic connection between microcosm and macrocosm, he drew up a reference system for magickal use. In *Liber 777*, Crowley adapted the Golden Dawn scale of correspondences and royal colour tables. This cross-references scales or series on separate planes. Planets are related to colours, jewels drugs, perfumes, plants, magical weapons, sacred alphabets and the tarot. Connected symbols may be combined to increase the occult dynamic. The actual use or symbolic representation of one item includes the dynamic force of a whole chain of connections. Anger also regards magickians as "a source of energy that reacts on other inert objects in a chain reaction"[4].

The film-maker references traditional correspondences in tandem with his personal mythology, by superimposition or cross-cutting. By including homeroticism, youth culture, fashions, countercultural stars, pop music and ironical humour, he extends Crowley's system, increasing its relevance for contemporary culture. Raymond Durgnat notes "the anomaly of ancient vision and rigorous modernity" in the texts[5]. An example of Anger's use of a symbol which operates on several planes is smoking, whether cigarettes, reefers or pipes. As well as signaling a hip style accessory or a narcotic, smoking also has the sacred connotation of "fire as phallic energy between the lips"[6].

The distinctions between Anger's source fits Crowley's use of binary oppositions and the dynamic play of contradiction to strengthen the magickian's independence. Contradiction is inherent in Anger's work. Filled with the apparent chaos of "disordering passions", it is also "scientifically cool and technically precise", constructed with deliberate care[7]. The dynamic clash of binaries extends to Anger's editing techniques. As Carel Rowe has indicated, Anger's parallel montages "form a complementary system of correspondences to Magick"[8].

The originator of montage editing theory (as opposed to the time-lapse montage method employed by Hollywood) was Russian filmmaker Sergei Eisenstein. He wanted a cinematic equivalent to the Marxist dialectical use of the formula: thesis plus antithesis equals synthesis. Eisenstein advocated art's function as "to make manifest the contradictions of Being. To form equitable views by stirring up contradictions within the spectator's mind, and to forge accurate intellectual concepts from the dynamic clash of opposing passions"[9]. Anger echoes Eisenstein's method, by using "the inception of new concepts and viewpoints in the conflict between customary conception and particular representation as dynamic – as a dynamisation of the 'traditional view' into a new one" (Rowe). In place of political analysis, Anger uses montage to debunk Christianity's emasculation of sexual energy. In *Scorpio Rising*, he intercuts the blasphemous rituals of the Hell's Angel Scorpio with a Sunday school "Jesus film", *The Road To Jerusalem*.

Talismans are a further technique from ceremonial magick designed to contact spirits. These include sigils, hieroglyphs, pictograms and most importantly tattoos, for their intimate imprint on the body of the practitioner. For Anger, these symbols act as "printed circuits" (Rowe) between the physical and metaphysical planes. He connects their potency with superstitions that photographs can steal the soul. Ultimately, the magickian seeks to establish contact and hold conversation with a personal Holy Guardian Angel.

To access deeper or higher levels, the magickian aims to "enflame" himself by various means. These include meditation, dance, music, incense and sexual stimulation. Ceremonial magick centres on rituals using implements, symbols and techniques relevant to the particular force being contacted, thus focusing the work. The adept's consciousness is thus tuned to the appropriate energy or deity and this charges the desired end. Invocation calls it down (or in) and is performed in a circle. Evocation calls it up (or out) into a triangle outside the circle. One significant difference between Anger's films and ritual magick is the lack of the spoken "words of power" which the magickian intones. His own work employs visuals and music instead, to release a potent visceral response in the spectator. The lack of language also throws the symbols into sharp relief and universalises them.

Ritualists employ a series of "magickal weapons" to access other planes. Among these are the traditional tools of wand, cup, sword and lamp. Wands, frequent in Anger's films, are emblems of will and creative energy traditionally gendered male. Anger has claimed the "cinematograph" as his personal "magickal weapon". His *Magick Lantern Cycle* works are "evocations and invocations" (Rowe) designed to spellbind the audience. Methods used to intensify psychic impact on audiences included the projection of red and green pentagrams at a Chicago Art Institute screening and the invitation to take an "acid break" during the programme's interval in Haight-Ashbury. His main aim is to introduce, illustrate and extend the work of magick.

References to Crowley's system permeate Anger's interviews and writings as well as the films themselves. The American edition of *Hollywood Babylon* (1975) is dedicated to the Scarlet Woman (Crowley's Babalon), and the flyleaf quotes "Every Man and Every Woman is a Star". This play with multiple meanings is typical of Anger's magickal reading of Hollywood's decadent allure. *Inauguration Of The Pleasure Dome* (1954) is dedicated "to the few; and to Aleister Crowley; and to the crowned and conquering child". This refers to Anger's fellow magickians and to Horus, the predicted catalyst of Crowley's New Aeon. *Scorpio Rising* (1963) includes a dedication to Anger's friend Jack Parsons, who was adopted by Crowley as his "magickal son"[10].

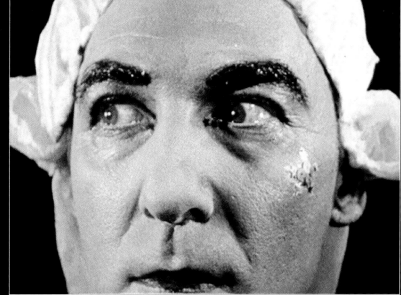

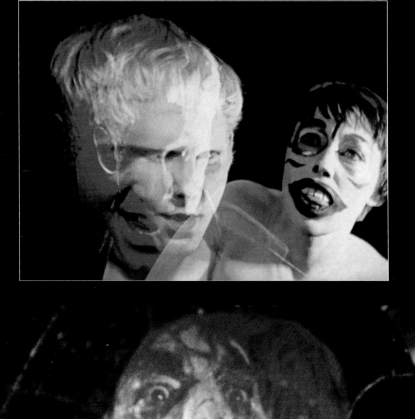

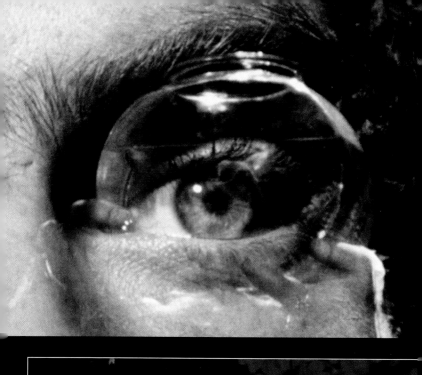

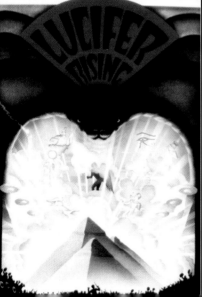

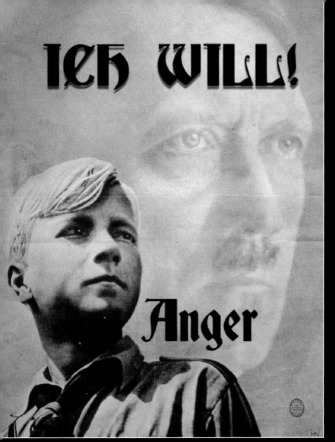

ICH WILL!

Anger

In his notes for 1966 screenings of the *Magick Lantern Cycle*, Anger presents an autobiographical outline[11]. This playfully describes his chief characteristic as a "left-handed fanatic craftsman"(a reference to left-hand path occultism). His religion is "Thelemite"; his deity is "Horus the Avenger" and his lifework is magick. His notes for the Cinema 16 catalogue detail Crowley references as keys to the interpretation of the films. *Eaux d'Artifice* (1949), a visual poem on water, for example, is prefaced by "Theorem V" from *Khaled Khan: The Heart Of The Master*: "Pour water on thyself: thus shalt thou be a Fountain to the Universe". Despite the esoteric knowledge in these references, it is possible for the spectator to enjoy the films without familiarity with Crowley. For Rebekah Wood, Crowley's work, as presented by Anger, is an open system, an "ordering in process, of infinite extension, not superstitious limitation"[12].

At the root of Crowley's magick is the belief in interconnecting spheres and fields of force, one of which is the magickian's will if used to maximum advantage in a fitting context. He asserts that "any required change may be effected by the application of the proper kind and degree of force in the proper manner, through the proper medium"[13]. According to Anger, his magick "avocation" is "like playing at something and having it become very real"[14]. He identifies symbols with their actual referents, and believes representations to be in direct link with reality. Whether sacred or profane, they can have a powerful effect on the spectator, both at conscious and unconscious levels. Metaphor at once stimulates the imagination and makes the occult (hidden) concretely manifest. Will Parfitt (in *The Living Qabalah*) has suggested that mages and symbols can be seen as both transformers and accumulators of psychic energy. As P. Adams Sitney suggests, Anger's work offers both religious revelation and "the dynamics of imaginary initiation" for both characters and spectators. The key power Anger sought to invoke through his cinema is Lucifer.

LUCIFER, LIGHT AND COLOUR

Light is a foundational mechanism of the cinema. It is also a chief mode of symbolic expression, especially on black and white stock. Anger's cinematography foregrounds light in all its forms. It glints, shimmers and gleams, enhancing colour tones in constantly shifting transformation. For Anger, an artist working in light, this is more than an expressionist technique. It is a manifestation of the power of Lucifer; the patron of filmmakers as "the god of light and colour"[15]. Indirect or overt celebration of this personified force can be seen throughout Anger's films.

Anger's view of Lucifer originates in Crowley and Gnosticism and rejects the Christian concept of the Devil. As well as being the rebel angel of the Aquarian age, he is also Puck, the spirit of mischief. Crowley's "Hymn To Lucifer" inspires *Lucifer Rising* (1970–81). Its last line "The Key of Joy is Disobedience" stresses human autonomy and freedom from repression[16]. It also suggests the realisation of our own godlike capacities, denied by Christianity.

In an interview with Jonas Mekas, Anger speaks of "the Fallen Angel, the fall from grace, and the hope of redemption, of climbing back up the ladder"[17]. As an acolyte of Lucifer, the "light behind the lens", Anger uses light as a magickal force in his films[18]. The sun, the earth's chief source of light and life, is a central symbol in many religions. Even the early Christians had difficulty distinguishing the rising sun from Christ, and St. Augustine cautions them against such confusion[19]. Crowley and Anger associate Lucifer with a form of solar-phallic worship.

Light simultaneously manifests and conceals the godhead. According to the Kabbalah, white brilliance is the colour of Kether, the highest sphere. It obscures God's presence from human sight whilst granting the illumination of the surrounding brilliance. Users of psychotropic drugs have likewise referenced light to describe ecstatic revelation. Aldous Huxley writes that "everything seen by those who visit the mind's antipodes is brilliantly illuminated and seems to shine from within"[20]. For Huxley, the contemplation of the luminous facets of a jewel or crystal is able to transport the user to "the other world of vision". In Ezekiel's account of a fallen angel in the Old Testament, the coloured lights of precious gemstones as well as white brilliance are used to describe his appearance before the fall : "Every precious stone was thy covering, the sardius, the topaz and the diamond, the beryl, the onyx and the jasper, the sapphire, the emerald and the carbuncle, and gold…thou wast upon the holy mountain of God; thou hast walked up and down in the midst of stones of fire"[21].

The dream narrative of *Fireworks* is motivated by the Dreamer (played by the filmmaker himself) going out to seek "a light" for his cigarette. Varieties of light in the film include firelight, a Roman candle, a Christmas tree and scratched film emulsion. *Eaux d'Artifice* (1953) is a visual ode in blue-tinted black and white to the sparkling of light on water jets built by the Cardinal d'Este in the Tivoli Gardens. Sequins and jewels on a dwarf's gown shimmer as s/he moves through the luminous garden. Slowly dissolving shots mimic the effect and movement of water itself, and the varied moods of light and shadow produce a hypnotic, dream-like effect. In *Puce Moment* (1949), coruscating light glistens off a series of coloured seqinned gowns moving in and out of focus alternately, allowing light to freely play upon their reflective surfaces. The final gown is black. Its sequins appear like stars in the night sky as the laughing lady mystically clothes herself in luminosity.

Inauguration Of The Pleasure Dome associates light with the precious stones swallowed by Shiva, who later eats a crystal pendant, a pearl and a gold snake. Such mixing of sight and taste recalls the experiments in synaesthesia by Baudelaire and other Symbolists. This process involves the extension and melding of the senses conditioned into five different spheres. As the jewels intrinsically possess light, the action of swallowing them suggests a talisman which only releases its power when ingested as food for the inner being. In Crowley's teachings, the oral ingestion of fluids in a sex-magick context deploys the absorption of supernatural force. This produces intoxication with the god until the body gradually purified by inner light. It is not sufficient to merely contemplate the light, but it must be consumed to be fully effective.

In *Invocation Of My Demon Brother* (1969), colours are generally bleached out and images overpowered by brightness. A red-robed deaconess bears a jewel-topped wand, a crystal ball gleams and a sudden globe of light bursts and rolls down the stairs. Anger as Magus is lit so that concentrated rays seem to appear from his head as he gyrates around his ritual circle. *Lucifer Rising* alternates solar and lunar energies, light and dark in a complex pattern of correspondences. Colours are saturated and their mystical associations more overt.

The colour scales in Crowley's tables partly derive from alchemical and Kabbalistic sources. They also draw on his studies of ancient Egypt, Hinduism and other systems which employ colour symbolically. Anger's palette employs multi-layered and complex correspondences which also invite subjective input from the viewer's subjective associations. The colours of the sephiroth (spheres) in the Kabbalah and the colours of alchemical stages are possible sources of Anger's choice of colour. Jung notes the metaphorical value of alchemy as a psychological model, and his studies stress "the signal connection between our modern psychology of the unconscious and alchemical symbolism"[22].

An example of Anger's metaphoric usage of colour is the use of lunar silver in the sequence when Lilith arises in *Lucifer Rising*. A further instance is the coquettish dwarf's suddenly green fan, which was hand-tinted in *Eaux d'Artifice*, used to signify both occult powers and the realm of Venus. The basic alchemical colours are black, white, yellow and red, although sometimes yellow is not included. In *Scorpio Rising* red, black and white, the colours evocative of Mars, Saturn and Pluto predominate. Their Kabbalistic associations include excitement, renovation, sanctification and admiration, as well as blood, danger, sex and death in modern culture. They also recall the Nazi adoption of the solar swastika on their flag.

As well as the symbolic usage of particular colours, Anger's themes might require the modification of shades and tones as the film progresses. One theme of *Inauguration Of The Pleasure Dome* is the end of the Age of Pisces. An oppressively decadent richness of colour is foregrounded, the hues being further saturated by the use of a black ground and shadows. Durgnat comments that during the film the colours darken "from shrill red and yellow to funereal purple, mauve and copper, to reflect the darkening and disintegration of the life-forms associated with a cosmic cycle, prior to a second cycle"[23]. Before moving on to more detailed analysis of particular films, exploration of the occult resonance of light and colour leads us into Anger's intentions towards the spectator.

ANGER AND THE AUDIENCE

Some spectators find Anger's films inaccessible or too demanding. Among those who enjoy them, many are drawn to watch them several times, each viewing revealing more and intensifying our involvement. Each time I watch them, I notice further details and cross-connections. This is partly due to their complex composition and editing, but I also notice, or register, extra flash-frames which can be missed if the viewer blinks. For some critics, the magickal elements remain in the background. David Curtis notes that for him, "some strange purpose seems to order the movements of the participants, but that is all" and that he is aware of rituals only at a secondary level[24]. Martin Scorsese, however, finds the mythical and ritual elements engineer a shift of consciousness. For him, there is "a pagan religiosity" in Anger's films, and "his continuous reference to myth and to ritual creates a hypnotising, a dream atmosphere that seems to put the viewer in a state of trance"[25].

Anger has explained his intentions in several interviews, stressing his aim to seduce viewers in "a transparent excuse for capturing people, the equivalent way of saying 'Come up and see my etchings'"[26]. He wants to engineer an altered state of consciousness and to "impose upon the mind of the watcher an alternative reality"[27]. For Anger, the mind's rational censor prevents his meaning from getting through. He refers to flash-frames or superimpositions of magickal symbols as "trademarks" for his product, explaining "these devices are barriers to the area of the mind that I want to block out: the Cartesian frontal framework. They're keys to get through to the great Collective Unconscious, in which I totally believe"[28].

Anger claimed that ideally, he would like to "project the images directly into people's heads"[29]. To create a climate conducive to spiritual revelation, he wants the spectator to forget that they are watching a film and "become one with the drama"[30]. The films themselves function as rituals which the audience attend, either as spectators or as participants. Anger's main aim is to induce affect at a deeper psychic level than aesthetic enjoyment.

Although Anger intends his films to be a more intense experience than cinematic entertainment, he includes humour and pop cultural references as well as rock soundtracks for the audience to enjoy on a variety of levels. Anger's involvement with rock bands led to appearances by the Rolling Stones, and Mick Jagger, who might have played Lucifer, composed and played the moog soundtrack to *Invocation Of My Demon Brother*[31]. Led Zeppelin's resident Crowley aficionado, Jimmy Page, composed the original soundtrack for *Lucifer Rising*. The viewer is also treated to the erotic pleasure of watching beautiful actors like Marianne Faithfull, Miriam Gibril and Donald Cammell, whose countercultural credentials resonate outside their film roles. There are multiple entrance points into the world of the films. As Wood comments, they are "never the impersonal, exclusively esoteric product of the secret society, but an order in which the spectator takes his place"[32]. I will now move on to looking at how the occult operates in several of Anger's films.

"FIREWORKS" (1947)

In his study of the American avant-garde, Sitney outlines a shift from the "trance" films of the post-war period, influenced by Surrealism, and the later "mythopoeic" films of both Anger and Maya Deren[33]. In Anger's earliest distributed film, the influence of Surrealism and Cocteau is evident in the use of sculpture and a wire mobile. The main action takes place in a luminous dream. On the mundane level, we witness a sado-masochistic, homophobic attack in the Gents lavatory. The underlying theme, however, is Crowleyan in inspiration: an initiate's symbolic death, rebirth and self-realisation. It has been linked by Robert Haller to the ritual of The Building of the Pyramid (*Liber Pyramidos*) in which the candidate undergoes a rigorous self-initiation. The Dreamer (played by Anger himself) seeks Lucifer as well as a light for his cigarette.

Throughout the film, Anger combines occultism with a knowing humour. The Dreamer seems to wake with a substantial erection, only to discover a pointed African statuette beneath the bedclothes. The finger snapped off a plaster hand and an empty book of matches suggests symbolic castration. When his chest is apparently torn open by his attackers, his exposed heart is a dial meter which stops ticking.

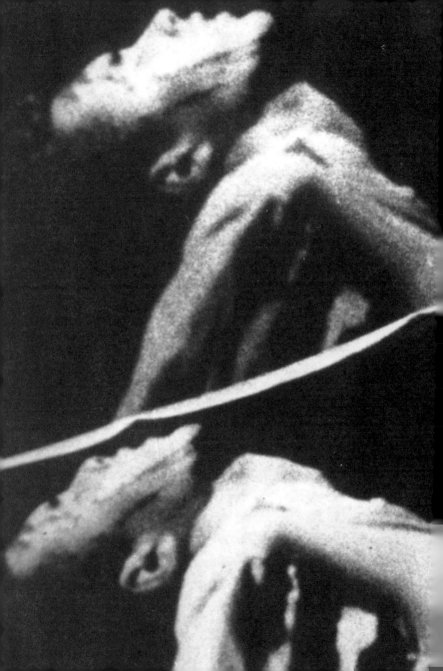

A sailor lights a Roman candle jutting out from his fly and ejaculates sparks of light. Street lamps are transformed into stars by blurred focus. Comic and satiric aspects in dynamic confrontation with each other illustrate "an art which argues with itself" and show "the simultaneity of the prophetic and satiric"[34] in the director's perspective.

The film opens with a shot of a torch extinguished by water, implying the temporary dousing of Lucifer's flame prior to rebirth. The Dreamer meets a sailor-angel in a bar. Rendered numinous by bright light, this ambivalent figure displays his potency by flexing his muscles. The focus on his back combines homoeroticism with a mystical reference from the Table of Correspondences. Here, the back corresponds to "the secret seed" and the muscular system to Horus, the Conquering Child. When asked for a light, he torments the Dreamer then offers him, invoking invisible word play, a flaming bundle of faggots.

After waiting in expectant darkness, the Dreamer is approached by a bunch of sailors bearing chains, which they use on him as scourges. As magickal weapons, scourges are used to arouse sluggish human nature. Chains bind wandering thoughts and signify dominion over darkness. Undergoing symbolic death, the Dreamer is revived by life-giving fluid: milk as sperm. The ritual closes with a naked stranger who joins the Dreamer, now back in bed. Initially he wears a glittering Christmas tree on his head, which juts at a phallic angle. In the fireplace, stills of the Dreamer in a sailor's arms are burning and peeling. This suggests his old identity being sloughed off. The tree is replaced by a head covered over by scratches of light, recalling the alchemical symbol of the sun-headed man. A final shot shows the Masonic emblems of a measure and triangle. The plaster hand now has all its fingers complete as the initiate's virile power is renewed.

"INAUGURATION OF THE PLEASURE DOME" (1954)

Inauguration Of The Pleasure Dome also mixes the sacred and profane. Originating in a fancy-dress masque where guests dressed as mythological deities, Anger's own performers engage in a decadent occult Eucharist. They are accompanied by the swelling organ notes and rapturous drumming of Janacek's *Glagolitic Mass* (1923) into which screaming is mixed. Here, the deities are given a Crowleyan slant, and feature Pan, Astarte, the Great Beast and the Scarlet Woman. They are joined by Cesare[35], the somnambulist from Robert Wiene's German Expressionist film *The Cabinet Of Dr. Caligari* (1922) and a changeling boy like the one played by Anger as a child. References to "strange drugs" feature strongly, from Coleridge's poem *Kubla Khan* which is evoked in the film's title, to Crowley's opium pipe, the Scarlet Woman's "big fat joint", and narcotic wine and powders[36]. Oral consumption is central and the Magus transforms all intake into spiritual essence. The porphyry cups, like wide-open flower calyxes, also suggest oral eroticism. As well as subjective hedonism, the narcotics induce a transpersonal

state for the characters, into which the spectator is drawn by cinematography.

Anger does not use a specific ritual, which would entail spoken word. Instead, he focuses on visual splendour and stirring music. He wants the viewer to be engaged by the progressive use of colour and fantasy which becomes "completely subjective – like when people take communion; and one sees it through their eyes"[37]. Shiva adopts different forms to receive each guest, becoming Osiris to Isis. He gradually induces the loss of individual identities as characters blend into each other and unite in him at the ritual's consummation. This mystic melding lends itself naturally to superimposition, the film's dominant technique. Previous material is superimposed on later shots, and footage from Lachmann's *Dante's Inferno* (1935) is overlaid. Flash-frame and superimposition add photographs of Crowley, the unicursal hexagram and alchemical symbols, such as the white lion and the red eagle. Shiva absorbs the essence of his guests by being superimposed over them. Watching the film, we experience the ecstatic breakdown of representation and linear narrative. This is cunningly engineered. Geometrically balanced sequences alternate with more chaotic shots. Compositions frequently place Shiva or his consort in a controlling position at the centre of other gods.

Anger's use of Tarot symbolism is frequent. Shiva's gestures as he manipulates the minor deities recall the Tarot of the Juggler or Magician. Intertextuality is shown by the

filmmaker's casting of bohemian writer of erotica Anais Nin as Astarte, goddess of the moon. Swinging her glittering mesh net she blurs our perspective and hypnotises us. The net references the pivotal Priestess card in Crowley's Thoth Tarot deck. In Waite's deck, like Anger's Astarte, she has a globe on her head representing the full moon. Anger's costuming of Nin also recalls Waite's description: "her vestments are flowing and gauzy and her mantle suggests light – a shimmering radiance"[38]. For Waite, she represents the supernal sphere Binah, as "the spiritual bride of the just man"[39]. In the film, focus is on Astarte's feet in black mesh stockings. The symbolic meaning of feet in the Correspondence Tables is "the elder witch", referring to one aspect of the triple goddess.

Light and colour are expressively used to indicate shifts in consciousness. Shiva changes colour several times, becoming purple, green and pink as he contains all colours within himself. A red shot of him laughing is followed by a white image in the lotus pose of calm contemplation. The mystical artist Marjorie Cameron, married to Jack Parsons, played the imperious Scarlet Woman[40]. Against a dark ground, in a black and white robe, her flaming red hair is thrown into relief, but a later shot shows her pallid, bleached out by the white light of ecstasy. Black and white squares recall the floor of Solomon's temple reproduced in ritual contexts. The contrasting elemental colours of blue and red are used for the eye in the triangle, a Masonic symbol of God's all-seeing unity.

Fire and flame imagery increases, to apocalyptic

effect, with the brassy sheen of infernal fires as the damned fall into an abyss. A thirteen-petalled sunflower in mandala form has golden petals round a vermilion centre. Golden light emanates from Shiva's hand in benediction. The predominance of fire at the end signals Anger's belief that the declining Piscean Age had to be destroyed before the New Aeon of Horus could be born. The lavish costumes, elaborate sets and gorgeously jewelled colours create the effect of stasis and a decadence turned in upon itself and drained of energy. Anger's next film would hasten the demise of Pisces much more forcibly by drawing on the growing power of youth culture.

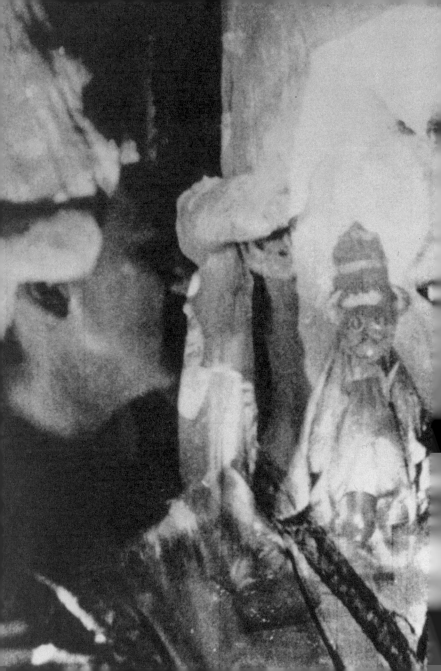

"SCORPIO RISING" (1963)

Scorpio Rising refers to Anger's own birth sign, aligned with the corresponding attribute of the imagination. The film's presiding planet is Mars and it foregrounds the aggressive phallic power destined to destroy the old system, being "a death mirror held up to American culture"[41]. The filmmaker's accompanying note asserts it as "a conjuration of the Presiding Princes, Angels and spirits of the Sphere of MARS, formed as a 'high' view of the Myth of the American Motorcyclist. The Power Machine seen as tribal totem, from toy to terror. Thanatos in chrome and black leather and bursting jeans". Material from contemporary youth culture has replaced the symbolist decadence of his previous film and it uses little traditional occult imagery on an overt level. It is, however, laden with magickal subtext. The complete replacement of old by modern forms underscores Anger's certainty that magick is fully operant in contemporary culture.

By using a pop music soundtrack, Anger opens up his work to a younger audience by the pre-existent allure of pop. Anger cites Crowley's endorsement of the power of words in "exhalting the consciousness of the magician to the proper pitch"[42]. The filmmaker deploys the song lyrics as ironical commentary on the visuals. "Blue Velvet" by Bobby Vinton changes both gender and fabric as it accompanies the erotic image of macho young bikers dressing in black leather. To the Crystals' "He's A Rebel", we see the contradictory, yet connected, juxtaposition of Jesus's miracles with Scorpio's

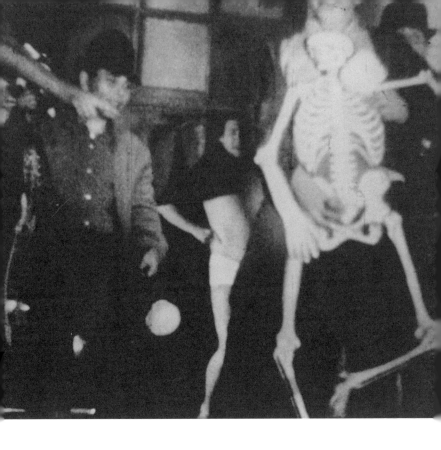

demonic agenda. Another new audience for Anger's films was the gay film circuit, attracted by the lavish, pin-up quality of the biker boys and the emphasis on torsos, tight jeans and erotic poses.

The first of the modern substitutes for traditional magickal weapons is the machine. As the biker fixes, polishes and prepares the gleaming bike, we are shown its aspects by slow, reverential camera movements. Lighting renders engine

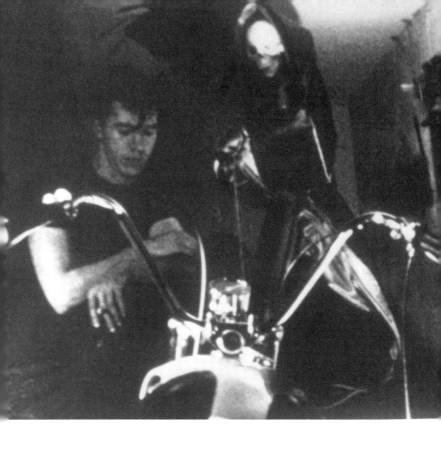

parts numinous as a beam flashes out from a chrome statuette
and wheel hubs suggest mandalas. Spanners and boots are laid
out like the Instruments of the Passion. The repair manual
glows as though it were a sacred text. Cigarette smoke rises
like wreaths of incense. Fetishistic worship also involves
fashion items, such as leathers, studs, rings and chains, with
their sadomasochistic associations, which may also be credited
with occult power by their users. Skeletons and skulls

proliferate in the bikers' iconography, underlining their flirtation with Thanatos. An alternative use of the skull is made when a poster of Death smoking a cigarette labelled "youth" is shown. Its initial meaning of youth burning itself out by excess is undermined when we see twin images of Jesus and a wholesome young man in its eye-sockets. The implication shifts to an attack on the Christian denial of the life force by preaching sublimation.

Anger uses the pre-existing iconography of the Hell's Angels' image and extends its already occult associations by developing and activating them. A hangman's noose decorating the ceiling suggests suicidal self-immolation, but also the hanged man of the Tarot. This card is associated with symbolic death and resurrection. The emblem of the scorpion features both within the diegesis and in flash-frame superimposition. Scorpio owns a patch embroidered with the arachnid. He also kisses his scorpion talisman before he leaves for the party to ensure success. Other beasts associated with Scorpio are the ill-omened owl emblem and his Siamese cat, presiding over his ingestion of the crystal meth as a kind of eucharist.

Comics, posters and TV broadcasts of films situate the events of the film within contemporary American youth culture. Playing both on the title of a Hemingway novel and the solar power of Lucifer, Scorpio is shown reading a comic strip titled "The Sons Also Rise". This further suggests the rebellion of 1960's youth against the values of their fathers' generation. Images of Marlon Brando and James Dean are foregrounded as components of his own image. Frequent cross-cutting between the film of *The Wild One* (1954) and Scorpio's actions highlights this. We see Brando effortlessly striking a match on his teeth, then Scorpio trying to do this with difficulty. As Brando's gang ride out, they appear to spur on Scorpio's own preparations as well as the start of the bike rally intercut as footage.

Other inter-textual references with occult implications are flash-frames of Hitler and a swastika-stamped game of drafts to suggest total domination as Scorpio sends out a death hex to the rally. Near the point of the crash, we have an image of Mickey Rooney as Puck from Max Reinhardt's *A Midsummer Night's Dream* (1935) who appears to be spurring the riders on to the fatal crash. Puck is associated with the juggler of the Tarot and also the Harlequin of Anger's *Rabbit's Moon* (1950) who maliciously teases Pierrot before making off with his beloved Columbine.

A key technique in Anger's attack on Christianity is the intercutting of the Sunday School Jesus film with blasphemous inversions. Anger's sophisticated cinema-tography and tongue-in-cheek humour ridicule the saccharine sentiment and low production values of *The Road To Jerusalem*. As Jesus walks into a house with his disciples, the bikers enter the party with obscene gestures, dressed in Halloween costumes as devils and skeletons. Jesus gets on his ass as the bikes take off. Jesus looks upward with a tortured expression whilst Brando also gazes up and pulls a pained face.

Brando is presented as more attractive and relevant to youth than Christ is. As polarised alternative forms of masculinity, each represents an extreme form which is incomplete and partial. Both belong to the Age of Pisces about to be superseded along with its patriarchal religions.

Blasphemous intercutting continues when a pious relief of Jesus's face follows a flash-frame of bare buttocks. On the altar, Scorpio pisses into his helmet as an inversion of the communion chalice whilst accompanied by the song "I Will Follow Him" and intercutting between Hitler and Jesus. In the Kabbalistic scheme, the kidneys and bladder represent "the ruler", so pissing is a magickal assertion of dominance as well as an insult. It also serves to reinforce the phallic and corporeal nature of paganism as opposed to Christian transcendentalism which seeks to deny the baser urges of the body.

The film ends with two deaths as a rider in the rally and a youth on the city streets both crash their bikes. A leather belt drops to the ground with "End" picked out in studs. Taking the ending literally might suggest a sadistic fantasy. In the occult scheme, however, death represents the symbolic death of initiation as an outgrown phase of life is left behind. The flashing red light of the police car could encapsulate both death and initiation.

On a wider scale, the death of Christian Pisces must be effected for Aquarius is to gain ascendancy. Crowley asserted that "the true Magick of Horus requires the passionate union of opposites"[43]. The film's mixture of binaries: sacred and profane; politics and religion; ancient and modern; piety and black magick, effects a process of levelling down. Eisensteinian cross-cutting forces the clash of opposites, creating a dynamic structural force. Both are needed before the New Aeon can come about. Youthful rebels such as the Hell's Angels mix the two primal, warring forces of Eros and Thanatos. Their culture of sex and death has sufficient occult power as an apocalyptic catalyst.

Later in the 1960's, when youthful rebellion had become more widespread, Anger was to extend his location of the occult within contemporary culture. The Hell's Angels are briefly seen at a rock festival in footage edited into *Invocation Of My Demon Brother*[44]. By the late 1960's they had been absorbed into what Anger regarded as the wider occult awakening of youth. Ironically, after Altamont, they could also be viewed as a force out of control, destroying Aquarius as well as Pisces.

"INVOCATION OF MY DEMON BROTHER" (1969)

The film as it now stands is based on fragments of a larger-scale unfinished work, a template from which *Lucifer Rising* was also produced. Its fragmentary nature is, however, its chief source of strength in mounting Anger's "attack on the sensorium"[45]. Viewers find this the most difficult of the *Magick Lantern* films. This is due to the rapid editing of confusing images, rarely on screen long enough to make meaning from them. Its visual flow is minimal, and for Tony Rayns "every cut hurts"[46]. The demands of watching are compounded by the endless repetition of a monotonously abrasive riff on the moog soundtrack. Sitney connects the chaos to the lack of a centre of gravity, so that every image has an equal weight and "the burden of synthesis falls upon the viewer"[47].

New techniques for undermining conscious control are introduced. The most striking of these is Vietnam footage of a helicopter setting down a troop of marines. Here, Anger printed one continuous loop of film on a C roll played simultaneously to the other two rolls. He has suggested that this image, which we only consciously register twice, is visible throughout the film with the help of infra-red glasses. The footage is intended to heighten the viewer's anxiety. Anger believes that audiences will sense the flow of men through the film, even when they are unable to see them. By this, the viewer's cognitive search for recognisable forms and patterns is blocked and the mastery of spectatorship is subverted. A more aggressive kind of magick is being worked upon the audience. As the ritual progresses, Sitney notes the increase of abstraction and anamorphosis[48]. This is the first use in Anger's work of an anamorphic lens for the kaleidescope effect of multiplying an image. This was a common technique to connote psychedelic states in the late 1960's. A more innovative effect is the ball of light which rushes downstairs after a ragged procession of musicians to announce "Zap – you're pregnant – that's witchcraft!" This enigmatic message could either imply the natural miracle of birth or the gestation of the Demon

Brother in a mortal mother.

The filmmaker himself returns to the screen in his most substantial role of Magus in a ritual to invoke the Demon Brother in "the Shadowing forth of Our Lord Lucifer, as the Powers of Darkness gather at a midnight mass". Anger's billowing robe acts as a screen for flickering movie images of apocalyptic scenes. For a magickian, the robe symbolises the aura. He gyrates widdershins (counter-clockwise) around the solar swastika[49] as "Swirling Spiral Force" to enable the

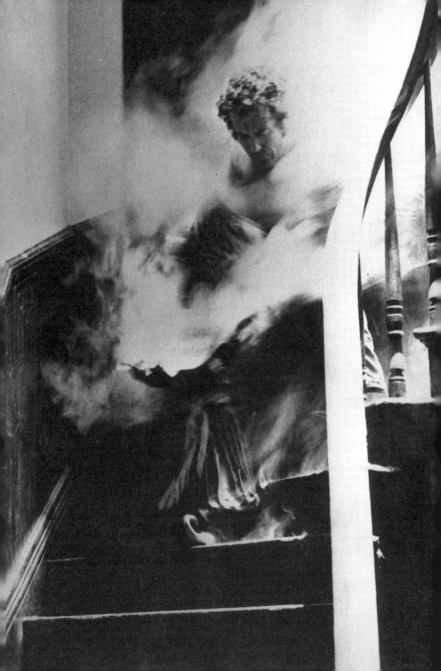

Bringer of Light to break through. In the Kabbalah, the swastika is an emblem of continuous spirit. Its symbolic use here as a flag is, however, difficult to dissociate from its historical deployment in the Nazi version of black magic. We have a close-up of the burning parchment held by Anger, as a magickal intention is sent out. To reinforce the spell, Hell's Angels and hippies dancing wildly at a festival are superimposed, along with Anton LaVey, founder of the Church of Satan in San Francisco. The potentially magickal effect of rock music and drugs on young people is underlined.

Recognisable people are used in the film to intensify its impact on the spectator. Crowley's influence is shown in a still of Anger reading *Moonchild*. His system is expanded here by the inclusion of LaVey. Jagger, Faithfull and members of the Stones are featured at the Hyde Park memorial concert for Brian Jones. Bobby Beausoleil plays Lucifer and his psychedelic band, The Magick Powerhouse Of Oz, is featured[50]. As with *Inauguration Of The Pleasure Dome*, Anger's own circle are used to personify aspects of his magick.

The occult agenda is fuelled by dynamic clashes and interrelations between symbolic emblems, chiefly the swastika, the circle and the pentagram (which appears in its political usage as a symbol of the US government painted on the 'copter and also on the Stars and Stripes flag). Other symbols featured are the arachnid tattoo; Crowley's sigil for sexual conjunction; the unicursal hexagram and the triangle. The three ball triangle appears both at the start and the end of the film.

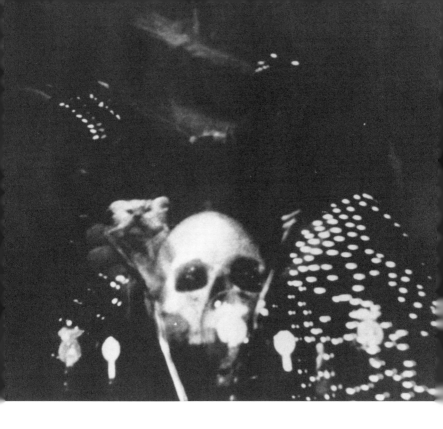

These are the supernal triad of the Sephiroth: Binah (understanding) Chockmah (wisdom) and Kether (pure spirit/union with god). The upward pointing triangle is the element of fire. It also symbolises the tendency of the universe to converge towards unity. In magick, it stands for a vision of the holy guardian angel.

The nature of the Demon Brother is ambivalent, with both angelic and demonic attributes. The opening shot is a luminous painting of the fallen Lucifer. Round his head are

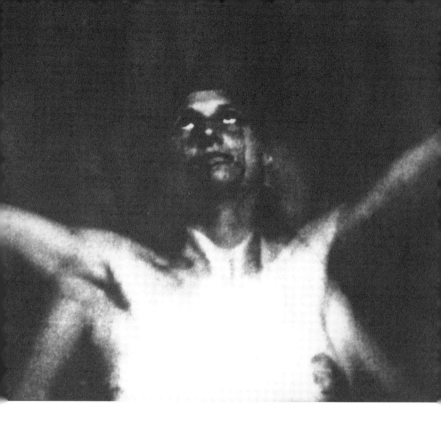

seven stars. Seven has mystical connotations on several levels. The Gnostic Sophia, goddess of wisdom, is crowned in seven stars. In medieval occultism, there are seven elements and seven planets, each with their gods. Lucifer has more mundane associations with the objects of Anger's desire, Beausoleil and Jagger. An avatar is the albino with glittering eyes, Speed Hacker, who raises a phallic crystal wand. In order to invoke the Demon Brother, blood sacrifice is hinted at. Early in the film, a man in lotus posture holds a knife to his breast. A cat

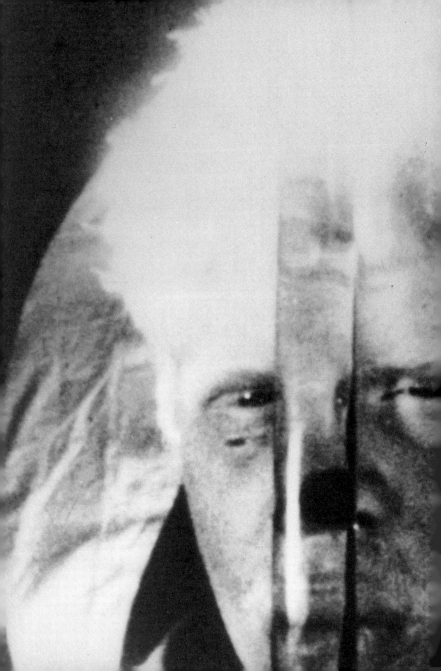

appears to be cast into a fire and there is a hanged man in tight jeans and cowboy boots. Anger as Magus baptises a goat figure in the centre of the circle.

Anger has described the film's "underlying background of violence and chaos"[51]. There are, however, associations and cross-references which provide a degree of structuring. An example of this is Anger's arachnid tattoo echoed later by a double image of a torso with multiple arms, resembling a Hindu deity. The playing-card-like double is also matched by an image of two young male lovers tangling together. The raised arms of a youth overlaid with a mesh of black lines fades into the three spheres of the final shot. Eyes are a striking motif, suggesting a presence watching and waiting. The albino's glassy eyes, a watcher hidden by a plant and an enlarged eye inside a crystal ball are examples. Solar associations are also frequent.

The film's abrasive impact on the spectator merits Anger's description of it as a "burn". If we are prepared to go with it, our usual mode of cognition is consigned to the flames. Anger defines his performance of the ritual, The Equinox of the Gods, at the Straight Theatre on Haight Street, San Francisco on September 21st, 1967, as belonging to "the last blast of Haight consciousness"[52]. As well as featuring in *Invocation Of My Demon Brother*, it was also the source of another film about "love demons" – which, in a very different style to *Invocation*, became Anger's most broadly accessible work.

"LUCIFER RISING" (1970–81)

Although it maintains a contemporary focus, *Lucifer Rising* is also a return to ancient mythology. It still uses dynamic clashes, but also features the alchemical "union of irreconcilables", connecting the elemental binaries of sun and moon, water and fire. Images of nature's power predominate, along with the ruins of ancient Egypt and visions of its re-animated gods. It is firmly within Crowley's world-view, geographically situated where he experienced a vision of the Angel Aiwass, source of the revelation of the *Book Of The Law* outside Cairo in 1904. As with all Anger's work, it is intended as a magickal working on the viewer, this time opening up a wider field of the sublime effects of nature and ancient history.

The cinematography reflects the sublime mood, with imposing long shots of landscapes and ancient sites. The identity of characters blends into their context and function. Anger explains, "I am trying to get away from identifying with actor or actress as a person. I want to move through nature, and the people are elements of nature also"[53]. By removing audience identification with psychologically rounded characters, the filmmaker draws us more directly into the forces they represent. This gives a sense of transcendence and transformation whilst "to command forces still not understood, we join them with a sense of dominion which is ecstatic"[54].

The film opens with the natural magic of volcanic eruptions and lava flows, manifesting the element of fire. Fire joins with sea, land and sky in an elemental conjunction to prepare for Lucifer's rise. The rising mud and the hatching egg of the crocodile suggest the Nile's fertility before Horus is born. Matching correspondences build up substantial chains of associations. No colours or objects are accidental. Visual rhymes are a key structural element in the overall grand design. Among these, we connect the sun in the sky and a volcano on earth; the opening eye of a crocodile and a mud bubble; an ankh carved in stone and the implement in the hand of Isis. Solar colours of saffron and gold predominate.

The juxtaposition of paired opposites is a portentous conjunction. Isis is paired with her consort, Osiris, then with her opposite, lunar Lilith. The realms of gods and humans are distinct, but they interconnect harmoniously, the magick of humans repeating and reinforcing the acts of the gods. We shift between divine and mortal in dizzying vertical edits which layer different planes or levels of existence. The mortal adept continues the conjurations of Isis and Osiris to herald the advent of their son. He lies on a solar saffron coverlet, like an Egyptian king in his robe of pyramid triangles. His numinous quality is evoked by a coloured aura round his head made of the trails of light he exhales. On rising, he sees a golden dawn, with its associations of Crowley's early training. The viewer's presence is acknowledged directly when we are beckoned to follow him into an inner sanctum.

The adept takes a bath after a ritual slaying. His blue and silver bathroom matches Lilith's tomb in the next scene. The soapsuds over his sinking face resemble the moon later

covered by clouds. His actions lead us to an interlinked plane where the lunar goddess awakens from a moon-shaped gleaming cave whilst the actual moon waxes brighter. Intercuts of bushfires and avalanches disturb the natural order as Lilith travels to Egypt and the home of solar Isis. Her pallid face and blue robe are anomalous in the bright sunlight. As the sun and moon conjoin, her robe is blown into a pyramid shape acknowledging the ascendancy of her sister goddess. Lilith is led by the light of seven torches to her conjurations, at Exersteine, the ancient site of moon worship in Germany.

After inserts of ancient sites, including Stonehenge and Avebury, we move on to the central ritual of the film. A candle-lit magick circle has been inscribed with the sacred names of Lucifer, Nuit, Hadit, Ra Hoor Kuit, Chaos, Babalon and Lilith. In super-imposition, a talismanic statue is thrown into water. The splash is suspended by slow motion which freezes the droplets into a crown. Incense rises as the Magus (played by Anger) descends the spiral stairs to converse with a sinister regal figure in an ermine cloak who has materialised within the circle. When the demon vanishes, we see bubbling mud, connoting abjection and the underworld. An elephant's foot crushes a snake, then a ball of smoky light shrinks and vanishes as evil is banished. A rapid intercut of Exersteine returns us to the circle as the music plays long, portentous chords which recall the film's opening theme.

A red, Masonic T square appears within the triangle at the centre of the circle as the Magus treads the circle deosil (sunwise) to a rapid, upbeat guitar riff with drums. A close-up focuses on his feet as he swirls at a supernatural speed, the vehicle of embodied force. An insert shows the visual rhyme of a whirlpool, then a swimming tiger. Intercutting is rapid and jerky as he creates a vortex which splits the screen inwards and the black space is torn by a zigzag of pink/blue jagged lines. A cone of energy is manifest, like a sharp spotlight beam. The Magus continues to spin, but the location has shifted outside space and time.

Lozenges of light fly around as the music climaxes.

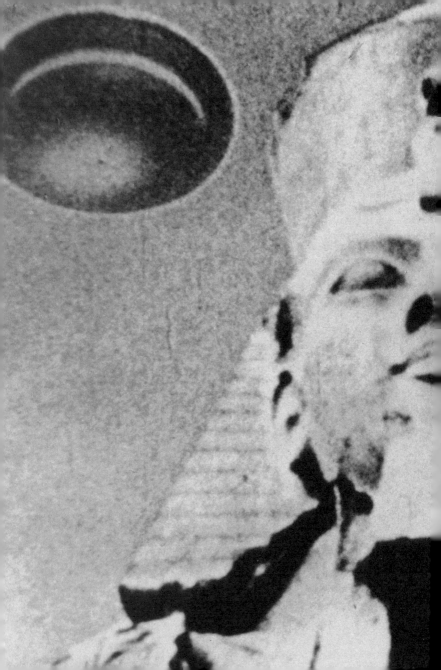

The white, red and blue light jags come directly at the camera, bombarding the spectator's gaze. They change from random floaters to spirals drawn like iron filings to the central cone. The Magus, clad in scarlet robe and pointed hat raises his arms as fiery red explodes. Smoke erupts, then a fiery fountain rises in volcanic spume. Lightning transmutes into rainbow-coloured beams embroidered, like Lucifer's name, on a boxer's satin robe. Lucifer slowly turns, and in extreme close-up his curls coruscate with red sun-glow, as his eyes look directly into the camera and out at us.

As well as the rituals and the ancient Egyptian context, other references to Crowley abound. A painting of a horned ram with lamp-like eyes suggests the Great Beast. Bestiality is further implied by an ancient Greek image of a satyr coupling with a goat. The acolyte pores over his reproduction of the Stele of Revealing, singled out for its magickal impact by Crowley as exhibit number 666 in the Cairo Museum[55]. In the background is a prominent photograph of Crowley, revealed behind a red cloth embroidered with an inverted pentagram. Other photographs of him, face-on, are briefly flashed.

Anger's use of popular cultural currency to broaden the appeal of his vision continues here. So do the in-references for counter-cultural cognoscenti. Donald Cammell, film director, occultist and reputed godson to Crowley, plays the green-tinted god Osiris, whilst his lover Miriam Gibril, is Isis. Lilith, acted by Marianne Faithfull, relinquishes her struggle and bows low before a poppy seed-head, which seems to be a reference to Faithfull's drug preference. The casting of Leslie Huggins as Lucifer reminds us of his mortal status as Anger's lover. The camp splendour of his attire is reinforced by a pink birthday cake decorated with space toys. The advent of the New Aeon is signalled by a science-fiction apparition of pink flying saucers. The final shot of the film returns to monumental grandeur with a long-held shot panorama of two Egyptian colossi as the gods, having completed their task, return to their ancient resting posture.

IN THEORY AND PRACTICE

Anger's techniques and images have had significant influence on subsequent film work. The interpretation of these texts, overlaid with mystical symbols and underpinned by magickal intent, eludes critique by existing cultural theories, although they can offer some inroad into understanding them.

The cinema in general employs occult (hidden) techniques to simulate physical manifestation. The Surrealist-influenced Antonin Artaud, writing in the 1920's, describes an occult model of cinema in which the physical excitement of rotating images communicates directly to the brain. The mind moves beyond the power of representation. For Artaud, "this virtual power of the images probes for hitherto unused possibilities in the depth of the mind. Essentially the cinema reveals a whole occult life with which it puts us directly into contact"[56]. For him, film is able to mainline into the

Unconscious. Some Surrealists made an uneasy marriage of Freud and the occult. Freud dismisses religious beliefs as an illusory psychic prop. For him, ego-inflation results from mistaken identification with the ego-ideal. With his roots in 1940's Surrealism, Anger's use of magick works outside the humanist paradigm of psychoanalysis.

Both Anger and his contemporary Deren produced Surrealist-style trance film in the 1940's then moved to alternative religions. Both share the basic Jungian perspective on the collective unconscious, itself based on extensive study of alchemy and ancient myth. Unlike Jung, who claimed a purely psychological interpretation of mysticism, both filmmakers were committed occult practitioners and high-level initiates. Like Jung, Anger's model compares mythic and religious systems, but his perspective is that of a believer. Unlike Jung's transcendentalism, Anger's system focuses on a celebration of the senses. It also references film, pop music, fashions, bathos and scurrilous humour, seeing magick at work everywhere.

Nietszche was highly regarded by Crowley as a Gnostic "saint". Nietszche's figure of Dionysus has some commonality with Horus and Lucifer. For Nietszche, the worship of an interiorised Dionysus brings joy and liberation, not repressive servitude. It is the religion of what he calls "the free-est, most cheerful and sublime souls"[57]. The myth of Dionysus, who is born, dies and is reborn twice is an emblem of the Eternal Return. Nietszche emphasises the god's non-identity, and the chaos of rapture engulfs the possessed worshipper's subjectivity in the embrace of "abysmal identity". Return to the self brings new strength and transformation.

Nietszche does not use Dionysian intoxication literally, but as a metaphor for aesthetic intoxication. According to him, we sample fictionalised excess by proxy as the rites of Dionysus are turned into objective images in an attempt to keep them at a safe distance. Apollonian form and restraint preserves our ego-boundaries. It distances us from excess by forming images outside the spectator's consciousness. At the same time, however, the spectator opens up his consciousness for penetration by excessive and disturbing representations. Emotional, even physical affect can be triggered by art forms such as film. Anger's art fuses Dionysian affect with tight formal structure. He does not intend to distance us by this, but to draw us further into his chosen system.

A more recent reworking of Nietszche is offered by the philosophy of Gilles Deleuze. Deleuze finds the psychoanalytical model too static, and inadequate to explain the processes of desire. In some respects, Anger's cinema fits Deleuze's search for an embodied aesthetics of force which melds mind, body and text. The filmmaker's work rejects verisimilitude and intellectualism, aiming instead for the material capture of both the demon and the spectator. Deleuze rejects straightforward representation for a more open process of "becoming". He describes film as process, flux, energy and plane of immanence, which mobilises and constructs newly configured desires[58].

Anger's work creates desire through the modulation and vibration of affect. In common with Deleuze, Anger privileges the visceral above the cerebral. He undermines the Cartesian dichotomy between body and mind as the "baser" urges of the libido becomes the centre of awareness. One major difference between their approaches is that Deleuze prefers an open-ended process of perpetual becoming. Anger, however, considers magick to be a solid structure on which to build a world-view, and does not seek an alternative path. Like Deleuze he seeks to replace the psychoanalytic notion of ecstasy by a more extendible model.

Anger's work has more in common with post-modernism than modernism. It refuses the modernist concept of alienation and loss by an alternative model, which pre-exists modernity. According to psychoanalyst Jacques Lacan, ecstasy or *jouissance* is beyond language, and temporarily fractures both individual subjectivity and the Symbolic Order[59]. This state is both simultaneously feared and desired. Afterwards, the subject returns to alienation. This is based on the psychoanalytic model of phallic ejaculation and post-orgasmic depletion. According to Lacan, the search for plenitude *(objet petit à)* seeks to compensate for the human condition of Lack. As with Freud's teaching, sexual desire is fraught with difficulty and often repeats infantile scenarios. In contrast, Anger's approach celebrates and extends *jouissance*, using it to empower the magickian.

Occultism seeks to extend immanent sensations and

teaches techniques for their development and retention. It was Anger's aim to use film as a magickal weapon, to effect change. As a magickian, he deploys a vital force interlinked with the "continuous phenomenon" of nature. As with Chaos Theory, also drawn upon by some recent branches of occultism (Chaos Magick), a change in one part affects the whole. The magickian's energy is charged by a variety of means, ranging from studying philosophy to the raising of *Kundalini* by Tantric sex.

Anger's films are both pre- and post-modern. They maintain the underground intent to disturb by content in tandem with the avant-garde purpose of undercutting customary modes of perception. They both glamourise and reinforce countercultural membership. As well as using cinematography to induce altered states, Anger's identification with the fallen angel Lucifer and homage to Crowley's decadent romanticism place his theology firmly in the underground as an aplogia for alternative religion.

NOTES

1. Other sources say Anger was introduced to Crowley by his friend and fellow underground filmmaker Curtis Harrington, who in 1951 bought him a copy of Crowley's biography, *The Great Beast* by John Symonds.

2. "[The Abbey of Thelema] was a one-storyed building of stone, plastered over and painted white, with a tiled roof, and walls of eighteen inches thick. Five rooms were planned around a central hall, the Sanctum Sanctorum, or the temple, of the Thelemite mysteries. On the red-tiled floor were painted a maigic circle and a pentagram, its five points touching equally the circumference. In the centre of the circle was the six-sided altar, which contained a copy of the stele of Ankh-f-n-Khonsu, with four candles on either side of it, *The Book Of The Law* with six candles either side, and other odds and ends... To the east of the circle, facing the candle-lit altar, was the throne of The Beast, and between his throne and the altar stood a burning charcoal brazier, hung with ritual daggers. The throne of the Scarlet Woman was in the west... On the walls of the temple and of other rooms in the Abbey were Crowley's own startling paintings of every kind of sexual act in every conceivable position." –John Symonds, *The Great Beast*, p152

3. Aleister Crowley, *Magick In Theory And Practice*, p.xiii.

4. Anger, quoted in Tony Rayns, "Dedication To Create Make Believe".

5. Raymond Durgnat, *Sexual Alienation In The Cinema*, p.60.

6. Raymond Durgnat, "Private Worlds".

7. Raymond Durgnat, *Sexual Alienation In The Cinema*, p.67.

8. See previous chapter.

9. Sergei Eisenstein, *Film Form And The Film Sense*, p46.

10. John Whiteside "Jack" Parsons was one of America's leading rocket scientists, as well as an occultist whose writings are collected in the book *Freedom Is A Two-Edged Sword.*

"...Parsons was the most dynamic American initiate of Aleister Crowley's OTO, although he broke with that society after the Beast's death in 1947. Parsons was that rare occultist who actually excelled in non-magical activities, pioneering the development of solid rocket fuel for the early aerospace industry. Parsons claimed to have conjured the Devil at the age of twelve, and a few years before his death he legally changed his name to Belarion Armiluss All Dajjal Antichrist, a sign of dedication to his spiritual mission. Years after his death, a lunar crater was named after him in honour of his scientific accomplishments. Appropriately, Parsons' crater is on the dark side of the moon..."

–Nikolas Schreck, *The Satanic Screen*, p81

Parsons died in an unexplained lab explosion in 1952, and many people believe his death was highly suspicious ("...Jack knew how to handle explosives, because he invented the jet fuel that took the rocket to the moon – so its unlikely he'd drop a bottle of nitroglycerine."

–Anger, quoted in Rebekah Wood, "Flames In The Night").

11.

Sun Sign: Aquarian

Rising Sign: Scorpio

Ruling Planet: Uranus

Energy Component: Mars In Taurus

Type: Fixed Air

Lifework: MAGICK

Magical Weapon: Cinematograph

Religion: Thelemite

Deity: Horus the Avenger; The Crowned and Conquering Child

Magical Motto: "Force and Fire'

Holy Guardian Angel: MI-CA-EL

Affinity: Geburah

Familiar: Mongoose

Antipathy: Saturn and all His Works

Characteristic: Left-handed fanatic craftsman

Politics: Reunion with England

Hobbies: Hexing enemies; tap dancing; Astral projection; travel; talisman manufacture; Astrology; Tarot Cards; Collage

Heroes: Flash Gordon; Lautréamont; William Beckford; Méliès; Alfred C. Kinsey; Aleister Crowley

Library: Big Little Books; L. Frank Baum; M.P. Shiel; Aleister Crowley

Sightings: Several saucers; the most recent a lode-craft over Hayes and Harlington, England, February 1966

Ambitions: Many, many, many more films; Space travel

Magical numbers: 11; 31; 93[13]

12. "Notes On The Hidden Cinema Of Anger Anger" p.61.

13. Aleister Crowley, *Magick In Theory And Practice*, p.63.

14. Anger, quoted in Wood, "Flames In The Night", p.51.

15. Anger, quoted in Wood, "Flames In The Night", p.52.

16. For further details see *Flowers From Hell – A Satanic Reader* by Nikolas Schreck (Creation Books, 2001).

17. Quoted in "Movie Journal", *Village Voice* May 1973, p89.

18. Anger, 1976.

19. See Carl Gustav Jung, *Psychology And Alchemy*, p.84.

20. *The Doors Of Perception / Heaven And Hell*, p.59.

21. Chapter 28, vv.13–15.

Anger was apparently drawn to Tivoli by the legend of the teenage Cardinal d'Este: "...Anger enjoyed a perverse identification with this 16th-century sex magick cultist.

"Anger calls d'Este 'a sexual pervert. There are very few things I call sexual perversion, but he liked to fuck goats, and that is technically a perversion... I think he was secretly a devil worshipper. Fucking goats is something associated with Satanism. The goat is like a beast of the devil.'

"D'Este's other kink was watersports. 'He liked being pissed on', Anger says. '...so the whole garden is actually a private dirty joke. It has ten thousand fountains and everything is pissing on everything else and it's like inexhaustible piss. There are sphinxes pissing out of their tits, which I think is wonderful. He used to throw orgies in this garden at night, lasting all night, lit by torches.'" –Bill Landis, *Anger*, p.63

22. *Psychology And Alchemy*, p.37.

23. Raymond Durgnat, "Private Worlds".

24. David Curtis, *Experimental Cinema: A Fifty-Year Evolution*, p55.

25. Martin Scorsese, quoted in Jayne Pilling & Mike O'Pray, *Into The Pleasure Dome*, p.55.

26. Quoted in Tony Rayns, "Anger Kompendium".

27. Quoted in Tony Rayns, "Dedication to Create Make Believe".

28. Quoted in Tony Rayns, "Dedication to Create Make Believe".

29. Quoted in Sitney, *Visionary Film*, p.123.

30. Quoted in Sitney, *Visionary Film*, p.25.

31. "The Rolling Stones' mind-blown 1967 manifesto *Their Satanic Majesties Request* had already illustrated the dark direction they were taking... One of their more successful groupies, the sinister beauty Anita Pallenberg, scion of an aristocratic family, had introduced the Rolling Stones' doomed bassist Brian Jones to her Satanic practise. Pallenberg... would go on to appear as an ambisexual seductress in 1968's *Performanc*e (released in 1970) alongside Mick Jagger. The latter, disturbing film was co-directed by Donald Cammell, whose father was the poet Charles Richard Cammell, a one-time associate of Crowley in the thirties.

"Donald Cammell's reminiscences of being bounced on an avuncular Great Beast's knees as a lad earned him a certain amount of cachet in Luciferian London, as well as the role of Osiris in fellow Thelemite Kenneth Anger's *Lucifer Rising*.

As Brian Jones drifted into narcotic oblivion, Pallenberg shared her witchy charms with Mick Jagger and Keith Richard, who subsequently went through their own dilettantism with diabolism. It was into this climate that temperamental Crowleyite film-maker Kenneth Anger drifted, promising to be the Rolling Stones' tutelary Magus. Anita Pallenberg was particularly impressed with Anger's reputation as a sorcerer. Jagger, flirting with film himself, was intrigued with what he heard of Anger's latest opus in progress, known as *Lucifer Rising*, which had already gained the reputation of being a cursed film. The legend of *Lucifer Rising*'s bad vibes fascinated Pallenberg and Jagger..."

–Nikolas Schreck, *The Satanic Screen*, p130.

32. "Notes On The Hidden Cinema Of Kenneth Anger" p.57.

33. Sitney, *Visionary Film*, p.123

Jean Cocteau (1889–1963) is the filmmaker with whom Anger is most closely associated. It was through Cocteau's auspices that Anger moved to Paris in 1950. Apart from certain similarities between *Fireworks* and Cocteau's *Blood Of A Poet* (Raymond Durgnat calls the former a "brutal demystification" of the latter), Stephen Dwoskin has noted the connection between the motorcycle ride as ritual ride of death in *Scorpio Rising* and Cocteau's portrayal of black-clad motorcyclists as the guides to Hell in his seminal film *Orphée* (1950). Both filmmakers have utilised myth, ritual and homo-erotic imagery to conjure visual poetry from the elements of an aesthetic quest.

34. Sitney, p.100.

Fireworks was one of the most blatantly homoerotic films yet made. Apart from its use of sailors – male sex fantasy figures popular in such magazines of the time as *Physique Pictorial* – and its S/M overtones and phallic imagery, the film also includes a subliminal shot of an erect penis. Before Anger's film, homo-sexuality had only been evoked, more coyly, in such underground productions as *Lot In Sodom* (1934) or Willard Maas' *Images In The Snow* (1943–48). Anger claims *Fireworks* to have influenced Jean Genet's gay classic *Un Chant d'Amour* (1950), perhaps justifiably.

Anger would repeat these homoerotic elements in the "male bonding" scenes of *Scorpio Rising*, which also includes flash-shots of erections and implied fellatio. Along with the likes of Jack Smith's *Flaming Creatures*, *Scorpio* helped pave the way for the gay porno movies of the late '60s/early '70s, including the bizarre films of Fred Halsted (e.g. *Sex Garage*, 1971) and James Bidgood's *Pink Narcissus* (1971), as well as the films of John Waters.

35. "Anger's shot of Cesare in black gliding past yellow candles anticipates Corman's Poe, whose aesthetic is also associated with a narcissistic, magic

and sado-masochistic thematic... pulp fiction and the avant-garde ally themselves to a perpetuation of the Romantic and Symbolist traditions."

– Durgnat, "Private Worlds".

36. "Although no one was taking drugs on the set, narcotics, as an active ingredient in psychic transformation, were central to the evolution of the film. A hallucinogenic quality informed the overall sense of visual style primarily via the employment of lavish superimposition. At one point The Great Beast gives Marjorie Cameron – The Scarlet Woman – a large joint which she sensually and deeply inhales. Later a powder with aphrodisiac properties that Lord Shiva had hidden in the chamber of his ring is put into a large chalice containing the potion – or psychedelic witches' brew as author Michael Starks describes it – an unspecified concoction that probably contained Yage, an age-old hallucinogenic used in ancient South American Indian rituals."

–Jack Stevenson, *Addicted*

37. Anger, quoted in Bruce Martin & Joe Medjuck, "Kenneth Anger".

38. Arthur Edward Waite, *The Pictorial Key To The Tarot*, p.76.

39. Arthur Edward Waite, *The Pictorial Key To The Tarot*, p.77.

"The film is derived from one of Crowley's dramatic rituals where people in the cult assume the identity of a god or goddess. In other words, it's the equivalent of a masquerade party – they plan this for a whole year and on All Sabbaths Eve they come as the gods and goddesses that they have identified with and the whole thing is like an improvised happening.

This is the actual thing the film is based on. In which the gods and goddesses interact and in *Inauguration Of The Pleasure Dome* it's the legend of Bacchus that's the pivotal thing and it ends with the God being torn to pieces by the Bacchantes. This is the underlying thing. But rather than using a specific ritual, which would entail quite a lot of the spoken word as ritual does, I wanted to create a feeling of being carried into a world of wonder. And the use of color and phantasy is progressive; in other words, it expands, it becomes completely subjective – like when people take communion, and one sees it through their eyes."

–Anger, quoted in Bruce Martin & Joe Medjuck, "Kenneth Anger"

40. "Parsons met Cameron under unusual circumstances, as might be expected with two such unusual beings. In 1946, he and a magical associate performed a ritual known as the Babalon Working, which sought to summon an elemental spirit representing the Whore of Babylon, the Scarlet Woman of myth. Shortly thereafter, Cameron answered an advertisement for a room to let that Parsons was offering at his Pasadena mansion. He interpreted her as the manifestation of the Scarlet Woman, and the couple enthusiastically took

up the practice of sex magic designed to give birth to a moonchild, a form of homunculus... Anger was fascinated with the occult legend that was already forming around Cameron, and his inclusion of her in his film was a deliberate connection to the magical climate created by the Babalon Working. Cameron's charismatic screen presence can also be seen in Curtis Harrington's atmospheric short film *The Wormwood Star* (1956), in which the Scarlet Woman displays a series of her esoteric paintings to the camera shortly before she destroys them. Harrington, who appears in *Inauguration* as Cesare the somnambulist, would return to this magical muse in the '60s."

–Nikolas Schreck, *The Satanic Screen*, p81

41. Sitney, *Visionary Film*, p.115.

42. Crowley, *Magick In Theory And Practice*, p.115.

As well as unveiling a trail-blazing use of pop soundtracking and pushing at the limits of screen censorship, *Scorpio Rising* can also be seen as paving the way for the deluge of "Hell's Angels" movies which swamped Hollywood in the latter half of the '60s. The first of these was Roger Corman's *Wild Angels* (1966), followed quickly by the likes of *Devil's Angels* (1967), *Hell's Angels On Wheels* (1967), and *Satan's Sadists* (1969). Apart from lashings of violence and metal machine fetishism, these films usually featured a *Scorpio*-style drunken/drugged orgy (though without the explicit sexuality), and are notable for the luridly Luciferian imagery of their titles.

43. Anger, quoted in "Anger Rising".

44. This footage is of English Hell's Angels, shot at Hyde Park during the Rolling Stones concert held on July 5, 1969. It was an American chapter of the Angels who, led by Sonny Barger, caused havoc at the Stones' next outdoor concert at Altamont Speedway, December 1969, where a black spectator was knifed to death. The concert was captured on film by the Maysles Brothers in their classic documentary, *Gimme Shelter*. Anger's connection to the Stones thus linked him to one of two fatal events which heralded the death of '60s optimism. The other link was Bobby Beausoleil who, after a relationship with Anger, hooked up with Charles Manson. Both the Stones and Beausoleil appear in Anger's *Invocation*, the decade's key occult visual coda.

45. Anger, quoted in Tony Rayns, *Anger Kompendium*.

46. Rayns, *Anger Kompendium*.

47. Sitney, *Visionary Film*, p.131.

48. Sitney, *Visionary Film*, p.132.

49. "...a psychic power pack... Hitler couldn't have done it without the swastika" (Anger, quoted in Tony Rayns, *Anger Kompendium*).

The imagistic power of Nazism stills holds a deep fascination for

Anger. In *Necronomicon 4* (2001), an article entitled "Kenneth Anger – Welcome To The Pleasure Dome" reports the screening of a rough cut of Anger's then-latest film, *A Hitler Youth's Dream* (later retitled *Ich Will!*). Anger is quoted as describing the film's conclusion: "I end the film with the winter solstice configuration where thousands of torches make up a revolving swastika when seen from above" (p.64).

50. "Beausoleil was a young man who possessed some skill in music and songwriting and more than a passing interest in devil worship and magic. In 1967 he was associated with famed author and weir-warped filmmaker Kenneth Anger in San Francisco. Beausoleil evidently lived with Anger in an old house in San Francisco called the Russian Embassy, where Anger introduced him to the universe of magic, not to mention the cruelty-streaked universe of Aleister Crowley. Anger was involved in making an occult movie called *Lucifer Rising* in which Beausoleil played the role of Lucifer. At that time Beausoleil has said that he was on an all-meat diet and believed himself to be the devil. Beausoleil was the lead guitarist and sitarist for The Magick Powerhouse Of Oz, an 11-piece rock ensemble formed by Kenneth Anger to perform the music for *Lucifer Rising*."

–Ed Sanders, *The Family*, p.42–43.

By October 1967 Beausoleil had split with Anger and was living with Gary Hinman, who supplied drugs to Charles Manson and his Family. Beausoleil inevitably became embroiled with Manson. On July 25, 1969, several Family members, including Beausoleil, were at Hinman's house to extort money. Hinman was killed and Beausoleil tried (twice) for the murder. In April 1970 he was found guilty and spent 2 years on Death Row until California abolished the death penalty.

51. Quoted in Rebekah Wood, "Flames In The Night".

52. Quoted in Tony Rayns, "Elusive Lucifer".

53. Quoted in Robert Haller, 'Kenneth Anger".

54. Quoted in Robert Haller, 'Kenneth Anger".

55. "'Who is Horus?' asked Crowley. Rose knew nothing of Egyptology. On her lips the name of Horus was most perplexing. For an answer she took him to the Cairo Museum, which they had not previously visited. They passed by several images of Horus, and went upstairs. In the distance was a glass case, too far off for its contents to be recognized.

'There!' cried Rose, 'there He is!'

Brother Perdurabo advanced to the case. There was the image of Horus in the form of Ra-Hoor-Khuit painted upon a wooden stele of the 26th dynasty.

Suddenly Crowley fell back in amazement: *the exhibit bore the number 666!* His number, the number of The Beast!"

     –John Symonds, *The Great Beast*, p.58.

56. Antonin Artaud, *Collected Works Volume 3*, p.65–66.
57. Martin Heidegger, *Nietzsche, Volume 2*, p.94.
58. See Deleuze, *A Thousand Plateaux: Capitalism And Schizophrenia.*
59. See Lacan, "God And The *Jouissance* Of The Woman".

THE FIRE/LIGHT TRIP

1. EARLY FILMS

Although *Fireworks* (1947) is Kenneth Anger's earliest film in distribution, and possibly his earliest extant work[1], the director apparently made a series of prototypes as a boy[2]. In *Film Culture 31* (Winter 1963/4), Anger describes these early endeavours as follows:

WHO HAS BEEN ROCKING MY DREAMBOAT (1941)

7 min. 16mm. B&W. Silent. Filmed in Santa Monica, California.

Credits: Conceived, Directed, Photographed and Edited by Kenneth Anger. Cast: A dozen contemporaries recruited from the neighbourhood. Synopsis: A montage of American children at play, drifting and dreaming, in the last summer before Pearl Harbour. Flash cuts of newsreel holocaust dart across their reverie. Fog invades the playground; the children dropping in mock death to make a misty landscape of dreamers.

TINSEL TREE (1941–42)

3 min. 16mm. B&W. Hand-tinted. Silent. Filmed in Santa Monica.

Credits: Conceived, Directed, Photographed and Edited by Kenneth Anger. Cast: A Christmas Tree. Synopsis: The ritual dressing and destruction of the Christmas Tree. Close-ups as the branches are laden with baubles, draped with garlands, tossed with tinsel. Cut to the stripped discarded tree as it bursts into brief furious flames (hand-tinted gold-scarlet) to leave a charred skeleton.

PRISONER OF MARS (1942)

11 min. 16mm. B&W. Silent. Filmed in Santa Monica.

Credits: Conceived, Directed, Photographed and Edited by Kenneth Anger. Camera Assistant: Charles Vreeland. Settings, Miniatures, and Costume Designed and Executed by Kenneth Anger. Cast: Kenneth Anger (The Boy-Elect from Earth). Synopsis: Science-Fiction rendering of the Minotaur myth. A "chosen" adolescent of the future is rocketed to Mars where he awakens in a labyrinth littered with the bones of his predecessors. Formal use of serial chapter aesthetic: begins and ends in a predicament.

THE NEST (1943)

20 min. 16mm. B&W. Silent. Filmed in Santa Monica, Westwood and Beverly Hills.

Credits: Conceived, Directed, Photographed and Edited by Kenneth Anger. Cast: Bob Jones (Brother); Jo Whittaker (Sister); Dare Harris –later known as John Derek in Hollywood– (Boy Friend). Synopsis: A brother and sister relate to mirrors and each other until a third party breaks the balance; seducing both into violence. Ablutions and the acts of dressing and making-up observed as magic rite. The binding spell of the sister-sorceress is banished by the brother who walks out.

ESCAPE EPISODE (1944)

35 min. 16mm. B&W. Silent. Filmed in Santa Monica and Hollywood.

Credits: Conceived, Directed, Photographed and Edited by Kenneth Anger. Cast: Marilyn Granas (The Girl); Bob Jones (The Boy); Nora Watson (The Guardian). Synopsis: Free rendering of the Andromeda myth. A crumbling, stucco-gothic sea-side monstrosity, serving as a Spiritualist Church. Imprisoned within, a girl at the mercy of a religious fanatic "dragon" awaits her deliverance by a beach-boy Perseus. Ultimately it is her own defiance which snaps the chain.

DRASTIC DEMISE (1945)

5 min. B&W. Silent. Filmed in Hollywood on V-J Day.

Credits: Photographed and Edited by Kenneth Anger. Cast: Anonymous street crowds. Synopsis: A free-wheeling hand-held camera-plunge into the hallucinatory reality of a hysterical Hollywood Boulevard crowd celebrating War's End. A mushrooming cloud makes a final commentary.

ESCAPE EPISODE (SOUND VERSION) (1946)

27 min. Music by Scriabin.

This shorter edition makes non-realistic use of bird wind and surf sounds, as well as Scriabin's "Poem Of Ecstasy" to heighten mood.

2. LOST, FRAGMENTED AND ABORTIVE FILMS

Kenneth Anger's film-making career has been marked by a series of films which were lost, stolen, destroyed, or abandoned due to lack of funds or other (often mysterious) circumstances. This pattern commenced soon after the completion of *Fireworks* when Anger failed to raise sufficient money to realise his next project, *Puce Women*, which was to be a feature-length film about fading Hollywood stars in their crumbling mansions. From trial footage shot in 1948, Anger was able to assemble and score a single fragment only, which he titled *Puce Moment*.

"*Puce Women* was my love affair with mythological Hollywood. A straight, heterosexual love affair, no bullshit, with all the great goddesses of the silent screen. They were to be filmed in their actual house; I was, in effect, filming ghosts." –Anger, quoted in Tony Rayns, "Dedication To Create Make Believe".

PUCE MOMENT (1949)

6 min. 35mm. Color. Sound (Music by Jonathan Halper). Filmed in Hollywood.
Credits: Conceived, Directed, Photographed and Edited by Kenneth Anger. Cast: Yvonne Marquis (Star).

THE LOVE THAT WHIRLS (1949)

Color (Kodachrome).
No credits available. Film destroyed by Eastman-Kodak developing plant, who objected to nudity in simulated Mexican fertility rites. "*The Love That Whirls* was inspired by Frazer's

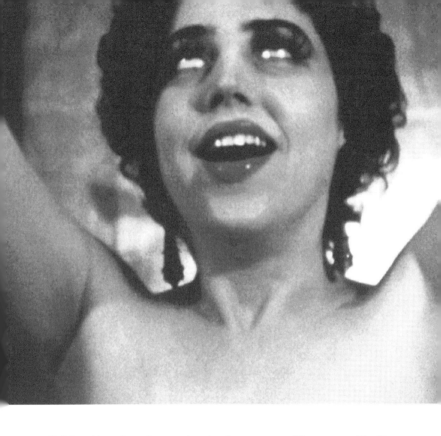

Golden Bough and was about a human sacrifice – specifically an Aztec ritual in which a youth is chosen to be king... After one year, the day comes when the King is sacrificed..." –Anger, quoted in Rebekah Wood, "Notes On The Hidden Cinema Of Kenneth Anger"

LE JEUNE HOMME ET LA MORT (1951)
16mm. B&W. Silent. Filmed in Paris. From the ballet by Jean Cocteau.

Cast: Jean Babilee (Young Man); Nathalie Philipart (Death).

In 1951, Anger essayed the first of three abortive Paris projects which underscored his affinity with decadent French art and literature: Cocteau's *Le Jeune Homme Et La Mort*, Lautréamont's *Maldoror*, and *L'Histoire d'O* (*The Story Of O*) by Pauline Réage. Anger filmed this 16mm pilot in the hope of raising funds for a 35mm technicolor version but, despite Cocteau's full support, he failed.

LES CHANTS DE MALDOROR (1951–2)

From the novel by Isidore Ducasse, Le Comte de Lautréamont (1868).

No other credits available. Tests shots only, of the early "hymn to the ocean" segment (employing members of Marquis de Cuevas ballet), and a war between flies and pins. In addition to the customary lack of funds, Anger reported being intimidated by the Surrealists who were wary of an American filming their most revered text.

THELEMA ABBEY (1955)

10 min. B&W. Sound. Filmed in Thelema Abbey, Cefalu, Sicily.

A documentary by Kenneth Anger on the erotic frescoes in Aleister Crowley's ruined temple. The film was produced for British magazine *Picture Post*, who "lost" the documentary.

Anger later described Crowley's paintings as "hyper-psychedelic murals: goblins and demons in fabulous colour, scarlet and pumpkin-red" (quoted in Rebekah Wood, "Notes On The Hidden Cinema Of Kenneth Anger")

L'HISTOIRE D'O (1961)

20 min. 16mm. B&W. Silent. Filmed in Paris. From the novel by Pauline Réage (1954).

Abandoned after Anger found out that money given to him by the boyfriend of the girl playing "O" was part of ransom paid out to kidnappers of Eric Peugeot, heir to the French automobile empire. It also transpired that the girl was the daughter of a priest, and when her parents heard about the film they immediately forbade her further participation. The story goes that the remaining footage is buried somewhere in France.

Anger returned to America in 1962 and, while living with underground film-makers Marie Menken and Willard Maas (Menken had directed the film dedication *Arabesque For Kenneth Anger* in 1961), made *Scorpio Rising*, his greatest success to date. As a result of the film's acclaim, Anger was awarded a $10,000 grant by the Ford Foundation – just before *Scorpio* was prosecuted for obscenity in Los Angeles. Part of this money went to the financing of Anger's next project, *Kustom Kar Kommandos*.

KUSTOM KAR KOMMANDOS (1964/5)

3 min. Color. Sound (Music by The Parris Sisters). Filmed in San Bernadino.

Cast: Sandy Trent (Car Customiser).

Fragment of an abandoned project. Failure to complete is attributed variously to lack of funds, Anger's nascent interest in psychedelia, and the death of the main actor in a drag race. Anger's original production notes read as follows:

"KUSTOM"

Film project by Kenneth Anger utilizing the Eastman rapid color emulsion Ektachrome ER, whose ASA rating of 125 opens up hitherto inaccessible realms of investigation in low-key color location work for the independent creative film-maker. Running time 30 minutes, track composed of pop music fragments combined with sync location-recorded sound effects and dialog.

KUSTOM is an oneiric vision of a contemporary American (and specifically Californian) teenage phenomenon, the world of the hot-rod and customized car. I emphasize the word "oneiric", as Kustom will not be a "documentary" covering the mechanical hopping-up and esthetic customizing of cars, but rather a dream-like probe into the psyche of the teenager for whom the "unique" aspect of the power-potentialized customized car represents a poetic extension of personality, an accessible means of wish-fulfilment. I will treat the custom cars created by the teenager and his adult mentors (such customizers as Ed Roth, Bill Cushenberry and George Barris, whose Kustom City in North Hollywood is a mecca of this world) as the objects of art – folk art if you prefer – that I consider them to be.

The aforementioned adult "mentors", most of whom are located in the periphery of Los Angeles and hence readily accessible for filming, will be shown at work in their body shops on various cars-in-the-process-of-becoming, in the role of "arch-priests" to the teenagers whose commission they are fulfilling. (The locales of body shops and garages will be presented uniquely in gleaming highlighted low-key, in a manner already essayed for the motorcycle garage locations of SCORPIO RISING); the idolized customizers (the only adults seen in the film) will be represented as shadowy, mysterious personages (priests or witch-doctors) while the objects of their creation, the cars, will bathe in a pool of multi-sourced (strictly non-realistic) light, an eye-magnet of nacreous color and gleaming curvilinear surfaces.

The treatment of the teenager in relation to his hot-rod or custom car (whether patiently and ingeniously fashioned by himself, as is usually the case, or commissioned according to his fantasy, for the economically favored) will bring out what I see as a definite "eroticization" of the automobile, in its dual aspect of narcissistic identification as virile power symbol and its more elusive role: seductive, attention-grabbing, gaudy or glittering mechanical mistress paraded for the benefit of his peers. (I am irresistably drawn to the comparison of these machines with an American cult-object of an earlier era, Mae West in her "Diamond Lil" impersonations of the Thirties).

The formal filmic construct of KUSTOM is planned as follows: (The division into titled "sections" is uniquely for working convenience; these divisions will be "erased" in the finished work.) The dominant pop record is indicated in capitals.

1 HAVE MONEY (The Young Conformers). An introduction insinuating the spectator into the teen-dream. A fast-shifting visual reverie utilizing the linking device of the lap-dissolve and the wipe to establish patterns of convention followed by the teenage (and sub-teen) group: similarity of hair-styling, style of dress, of language, attitude or manner, taste in dance patterns and pop music; the omniscience of certain popular heroes or ever-shifting masks on Archetypal Images.

2 DAWN (Crystalization). The concept of individual "style" dawns upon the Teenager. The carefully composed aerodynamics of a crested coiffure as it is formed. The love-lock. Raided sideburns. The embroidered, self-identifying jacket or painted T-shirt. The "far-out" color combinations in stove-pipe pants, shock-effect shirts and socks. The Grail: the vision of the Teenager as Owner of his own, screamingly individualistic, unique and personlized custom car. (These images of the Grail, "the goal", will be floated across the mirrored image of the Teenager as he arranges his coiffure or clothes.) Subliminal flashes as thumbs through hot-rod magazines or plays juke-box. Closeups of high-school desk tops showing open text books (Science or History) while adolescent hands doodle, first crudely, then with increasing refinement, silhouettes of hot-rod and custom "dream" cars.

3 THE NITTY-GRITTY (Realization). The Teenager attacks. Dream into action. Abrupt change in formal construct: sharp cuts, swift pans, darting dollies. The night-lit junk-yard, weird derelict cemetery: lifting a "goodie". The first jalopie: a rusty junked car pushed into the dark initiatory cave of the garbage. Series of car-framers in the process of being stripped: an almost savage dismantling (analogy to wild animals dismembering a carcass).

4 MY GUY (The Rite.) Under the occult guidance of the shadowy, mysterious adult customizers performing as Arch-Priest, the Teenager's Dream Car is born (allusion to obstetrics). The alchemical elements come into play: phosphorescent blue tongue of the welding flame, cherry glow of joins, spark shower of the buffer. Major operation: dropping the front, raising the back of the car, "channeling" and "chopping". The Priest-Surgeon (customizer) perfects the metal modulations from cardboard mock-ups; plunges in with blowtorch and mallet. The swooping sculpted forms (blackened and rough) materialize in closeups and their intent is perceived.

5 IN HIS KISS (The Adorning). Sudden darting color: the rainbow array as cans are opened, stirred dripping gaudy sticks held up for the Teenager's contemplation and approval. The iridescent "candy-flake" colors and shock-jewel tones in vogue. The Teenager chooses "his" color: tension, decision, joyful release. The cult-object – the shaping-up car body – in the swirl of colored spray-gun mists: rose and turquoise flourescent fogs as coat upon carefully-stroked, glittering coat, the car-body emerges as a radiant, gem-hued object of adoration. A reflected color-bath splashes over the absorbed faces of the watching teenagers: a whoop of triumph, a jungle-stomp of joy as the custom is "born".

6 WONDERFUL ONE (Possession). The Teenager takes possession of his own completed custom or hot-rod car: the painted finish is caressed, the line admired (as would be the line of a girl friend), the chromed shift fondled, firmly grasped. (For this kaleidoscopic montage involving scores of custom and hot-rod cars, it is hoped to include the outstanding examples of customizing currently touring America in the Ford Custom Car Caravan, which could well represent the ideal Dream Cars of America's custom-conscious teenagers. However, for their appearance in KUSTOM, it will be necessary to film them "in movement" against unified black or nocturnal backgrounds – an effect that can be accomplished by camera or optical artifice if it proves impractical to night-drive these valuable machines.)

7 THE FUGITIVE (Flight and Freedom). The Teenage hot-rodders "rev up" (The Syndrome of the Shift) and take off for a nocturnal drag race (irreal colored light-sources throughout). A lone hot-rodder races down a curving mountain road (Dead Man's Curve). The Custom Boys, "in slow motion", take command of the controls of their Dream Cars. (This concluding sequence of KUSTOM operates exclusively in the realm of "dream logic": it is intended to create a Science-Fictional atmosphere.) The hot-rodders experience the erotic power-ecstasy of the Shift (the Hurst shift will be employed) to the magnified accompaniment of motor and exhaust. The Custom Boys resemble Astronauts at their controls: their vari-hued craft seem to lift into space. (If possible, a prototype of an actual "air-car" by a noted West Coast designer will be utilized in this section.) The Dragsters streak down the search-light stabbed runway (ideally seen by helicopter) as in cross-cutting the Custom Boys are liberated into weightlessness with their strange craft, and plunge star-ward.

8 SHANGRI-LA (Apotheosis). The Dragsters streak towards an imposing podium (by montage inference) piled high with towering, animated trophies of glittering gold; the Custom Boys range above the golden mountain high and free. A nocturnal jostling cheering crowd of teenagers (lit by swinging stabbing searchlights) swing up on their shoulders The Winner – Mr. Hot-Rod, his glowing triumpth-filled countenance streaming sweat, his bare arms bearing his Golden Trophy Tower – he exults as The Conqueror, drinks in the adulation of the adolescent sea around him; he is startled by the sky-borne vroom of the upwards-sweeping Dream Cars, his beaming face swiftly mirroring, in the moment of his triumph, a greater wonder, a greater goal.

As funds for *Kustom Kar Kommandos* failed to materialize, Anger began to turn his attentions towards the burgeoning Haight-Ashbery scene in San Francisco, and the formulation of a new project: *Lucifer Rising*. (Anger was now living in Fulton Street, SF, in a mansion known as the "Russian Embassy".) Anger informed film critic Sheldon Renan that the film was to be his "first religious film", about a "holy" war between the Piscean Age (in decline) and the new, ascendent Age of Aquarius – epitomised by the conflict between kids and their parents, which was now escalating due to the advent of psychedelia. The casting of the film's protagonist produced some legendary tales. According to Anger, his first Lucifer was a 5-year-old boy named Godot, who killed himself trying to fly from a rooftop. He then met a "demonic" figure named Joe Lucifer, apparently summoned after Anger had performed Crowley's "Invocation of the Bornless One" in Golden Gate Park; this Lucifer disappeared after a few days, possibly returning to the insane asylum he had absconded from. Anger's next Lucifer was a certain Robert K. "Cupid" Beausoleil.[3]

LUCIFER RISING (A LOVE VISION) (1966)
1600 feet. Color. Filmed in San Francisco.
Cast: Bobby Beausoleil (Lucifer). No other details available. Edited footage stolen in 1967.

"It's a film about the Love Generation, but seen in depth – like the Fourth Dimension. It's about love – the violence as well as the tenderness... There's an invisible war going on... a war between the forces of life and death, love and hate.... I see the embodiment of love among the children as winning. Lucifer is actually a sunshine child..." –Anger, quoted in "Anger Rising"

Anger very publicly blamed the theft of *Lucifer* on Bobby Beausoleil, yet Beausoleil has always denied this, counter-claiming that Anger was in fact financially unable to reclaim his film from the processors; furthermore, he has suggested that the "theft" was in fact the first stage in an outrageous publicity stunt by Anger, the next part of which involved the filmmaker journeying to New York where, at the offices of

Jonas Mekas, he reputedly immolated reels of unreleased, irreplaceable film. At the same time he publicly renounced film-making, placing the following full-page, black-bordered artistic epitaph[4] in *The Village Voice*:

In Memoriam
Kenneth Anger
Film-Maker
1947–67

The next stage of Anger's trip took him to Washington D.C., where he joined in a massive anti-Vietnam protest march on the Pentagon in late October (the filmmaker had already criticized the Vietnam War, describing it as "the establishment's way of masturbating young boys' violence" in an interview published in the *Los Angeles Free Press* the previous year).[5] Kenneth Anger next surfaced in London in 1968, where he entered into his dalliance with Mick Jagger[6] and commenced plans to edit the cutting-room fragments of the 1966 *Lucifer Rising* together with new footage to construct *Invocation Of My Demon Brother*, before starting the brand new version of *Lucifer* which would prove to be his final major film.

3. COMPLETE FILMS

The core of Kenneth Anger's completed film work he collectively refers to as "The Magic Lantern Cycle". All credits and synopsis notes by Anger:

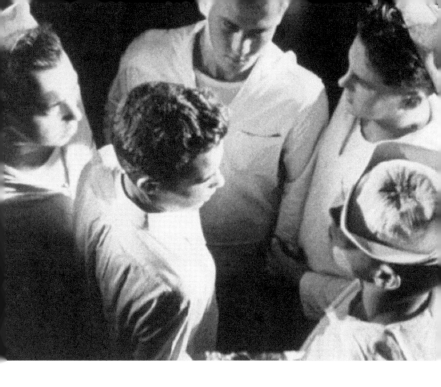

FIREWORKS (1947)

15 min. 16mm. B&W. Sound (Music by Respighi). Filmed in Hollywood.

Credits: Conceived, Directed, Photographed and Edited by Kenneth Anger. Camera Assistant: Chester Kessler. Cast: Kenneth Anger (The Dreamer); Bill Seltzer (Bare-Chested Sailor); Gordon Gray (Body-Bearing Sailor); crowd of sailors. Synopsis: A dissatisfied dreamer awakes, goes out in the night seeking "a light" and is drawn through the needle's eye. A dream of a dream, he returns to a bed less empty than before.

LA LUNE DES LAPINS (RABBIT'S MOON, 1950–79)

7 min. 35mm. Tinted B&W. Sound (Music by Andy Arthur). Filmed in Paris.

Credits: Conceived, Directed, Photographed and Edited by Kenneth Anger. Camera Assistant: Tourjansky. Cast: André Soubeyran (Pierrot), Claude Revenant (Harlequin), Nadine Valence (Columbine).

Synopsis: A lunar dream utilizing the classic pantomime figure of Pierrot in an encounter with a prankish, enchanted Magic Lantern.

Rabbit's Moon was the first film attempted by Anger after he moved from America to Paris in 1950 (largely due to the encouragement of Jean Cocteau, who had written to Anger praising his *Fireworks* as coming "from that beautiful night from which emerge all the true works"). Anger based himself there for the next decade, whilst travelling to such destinations as Egypt, Czechoslovakia, and Italy (where he filmed *Eaux d'Artifice*). Anger began to film *La Lune Des Lapins* in 1950, but soon ran out of resources. For 20 years the abandoned film languished in the vaults of the Cinémathèque Française. In 1972 Anger retrieved it and edited and released a 16-minute version from the extant footage, with a pop soundtrack featuring The Flamingos' "I Only Have Eyes For You", The Dells' "Oh, What A Night", The Capris' "There's A Moon Out Tonight", and Mary Wells' "Bye Bye Baby"; and in 1979 he released the present 7-minute version.

EAUX D'ARTIFICE (1953)

13 min. 16mm. Color. Sound (Music by Vivaldi). Filmed in the

Gardens of the Villa D'Este, Tivoli, by special permission of the Italian Department of Antiquities, on Ferrania Infra-Red. Printed on Ektachrome through a Cyan filter. The fan of Exorcism hand-tinted by Kenneth Anger with Spectra Color.

Credits: Conceived, Directed, Photographed, and Edited by Kenneth Anger. Assistant Camera: Thad Lovett. Cast: Carmillo Salvatorelli (The Water Witch). Synopsis: Hide and seek in a night-time labyrinth of levels, cascades, balustrades, grottoes, and ever-gushing, leaping fountains, until the Water Witch and the Fountain become One.

"Pour water on thyself: thus shalt thou be a Fountain to the universe. Find thou thyself in every Star! Achieve thou every possibility!"

–Khaled Khan*, The Heart Of The Master, Theorem V.*

Dedicated to Pavel Tchelitchev.

Anger has also described *Eaux d'Artifice* as "the evocation of a Firbank heroine", her flight the "pursuit of the night moth" (Sitney, p.102). Carmillo Salvatorelli was a circus dwarf of indistinct gender whom Anger met in Italy.

INAUGURATION OF THE PLEASURE DOME (1954–66)

38 min. Color. Sound (Music by Janacek). Filmed at Shiva's house, Hollywood, and another place. Printed by Kenneth Anger in Hand Lithography System on A,B,C,D, and e rolls, on Ektachrome 7387.

Credits: Conceived, Directed, Photographed, and Edited by Kenneth Anger. Assistant Camera: Robert Straede. Costumes, Lighting and Make-up by Kenneth Anger. Properties and Setting courtesy Samson de Brier. Cast: Samson de Brier

(Lord Shiva, Osiris, Cagliostro, Nero, The Great Beast 666); Cameron (The Scarlet Woman, Lady Kali); Kathryn Kadell (Isis); Renata Loome (Lilith); Anais Nin (Astarte); Kenneth Anger (Hecate); Peter Loome (Ganymede); Paul Mathison (Pan); Curtis Harrington (Cesare The Somnambulist); Joan Whitney (Aphrodite). Synopsis (*Sacred Mushroom Edition*): Lord Shiva, The Magician, wakes. A convocation of Theurgists in the guise of figures from mythology bearing gifts: The Scarlet Woman, Whore of Heaven, smokes a big fat joint; Astarte of the Moon brings the wings of snow; Pan bestows trhe bunch of Bacchus; Hecate offers the Sacred Mushroom, Yage, Wormwood Brew. The vintage of Hecate is poured: Pan's cup is poisoned by Lord Shiva. The *Orgia* ensues; a Magick masquerade party at which Pan is the prize. Lady Kali blesses the rites of the Children of the Light as Lord Shiva invokes the Godhead with the formula, *"Force and Fire"*.

"A Eucharist of some sort should most assuredly be consumed daily by every magician, and he should regard it as the main sustenance of his magical life. It is of more importance than any other magical ceremony, because it is a complete circle. The whole of the force expended is completely re-absorbed; yet the virtue is that vast gain represented by the abyss between Man and God.

"The magician becomes filled with God, fed upon God, intoxicated with God. Little by little his body will become purified by the internal lustration of God; day by day his mortal frame, shedding its earthly elements, will become the very truth of the Temple of the Holy Ghost. Day by day matter is replaced by Spirit, the human by the divine; ultimately the

change will be complete; God manifest in the flesh will be his name."

–The Master Therion (Aleister Crowley), *Magick In Theory And Practice.*

Dedicated to the Few, and to Aleister Crowley; and to the Crowned and Conquering Child.

Inauguration Of The Pleasure Dome has undergone several mutations; it is the definitive "Sacred Mushroom Edition" (1966) which remains in distribution. This version is soundtracked by Leos Janacek's Glagolitic Mass. The original version (1954–56) had music by the eccentric Harry Partch and was 41 minutes in length; a 1958 version was projected on 3 screens, with 3 acts entitled "The Talisman", "The Banquet Of Poisons", and "The Ceremonies Of Consummation". Anger also cut a 38-minute version in 1978, with music by the Electric Light Orchestra. The film's mutability is demonstrated by the different synopsis presented by Anger for a New York screening in 1956: "The Abbey of Thelema, the evening of the 'sunset' of Crowleyanity. Lord Shiva wakes. Madam Satan presents the mandragore, and a glamor is cast. A convocation of enchantresses and theurgists. The idol is fed. Aphrodite presents the apple; Isis presents the serpent. Astarte descends with the witch-ball, the Fairy Geffe takes wing. The gesture of the Juggler invokes the Tarot Cups. The Elixir of Hecate is served by the Somnambulist. Pan's drink is venomed by Lord Shiva. The enchantment of Pan. Astarte withdraws with the glistering net of Love. The arrival of the Secret Chief. The Ceremonies of Consummation are presided over by the Great Beast-Shiva and the Scarlet Woman-Kali."

SCORPIO RISING (1963)

29 min. Color. Sound (Music by Ricky Nelson, Little Peggy March, The Angels, Bobby Vinton, Elvis Presley, Ray Charles, The Crystals, The Ran-Dells, Kris Jensen, Claudine Clark, Gene McDaniels, The Surfaris). Filmed in Brooklyn, Manhattan, and Walden's Pond, New York, on Ektachrome ER.

Credits: Conceived, Directed, Photographed, and Edited by Kenneth Anger. Cast: Bruce Byron (Scorpio); Johnny Sapienza (Taurus); Frank Carifi (Leo); John Palone (Pinstripe); Ernie Allo (The Life Of The Party); Barry Rubin (Pledge); Steve Crandell (The Sissy Cyclist). Synopsis: A conjuration of the Presiding Princes, Angels, and Spirits of the Sphere of MARS, formed as a "high" view of the Myth of the American Motorcyclist. The Power Machine seen as a tribal totem, from toy to terror. Thanatos in chrome and black leather and bursting jeans. *Part I*: "Boys And Bolts" (masculine fascination with the Thing that Goes); *Part II*: "Image Maker" (getting high on heroes: Dean's Rebel and Brando's Johnny: the True View of J.C.); *Part III*: "Walpurgis Party" (J.C. wallflower at cycler's Sabbath); *Part IV*: "Rebel Rouser" (The Gathering of the Dark Legions, with a message from Our Sponsor).

"It may be conceded in any case that the long strings of formidable words which roar and moan through so many conjurations have a real effect in exalting the consciousness of the magician to the proper pitch – that they should do so is no more extraordinary than music of any kind should do so.

"Magicians have not confined themselves to the use of

the human voice. The pan-pipe with its seven stops, corresponding to the seven planets, the bull-roarer, the tom-tom, and even the violin, have all been used, as well as many others, of which the most important is the bell, though this is used not so much for actual conjuration as to mark stages in the ceremony. Of all these the tom-tom will be found the most generally useful."

–The Master Therion (Aleister Crowley), *Magick In Theory And Practice.*

Dedicated to Jack Parsons, Victor Childe, Jim Powers, James Dean, T.E. Lawrence, Hart Crane, Kurt Mann, The Society of Spartans, The Hell's Angels, and all overgrown boys who will ever follow the whistle of Love's brother.

INVOCATION OF MY DEMON BROTHER (1969)

11 min. Color. Sound (Music composed by Mick Jagger on the Moog Synthesizer). Filmed in San Francisco at the Straight Theatre and the Russian Embassy.

Credits: Conceived, Directed, Photographed, and Edited by Kenneth Anger. Cast: Speed Hacker (Wand Bearer); Lenore Kandel and William (Deaconess and Deacon); Kenneth Anger (The Magus); Van Leuven (Acolyte); Harvey Bialy and Timotha (Brother and Sister of the Rainbow); Anton Szandor LaVey (His Satanic Majesty); Bobby Beausoleil (Lucifer). Synopsis: Invocation of My Demon Brother (Arrangement in Black and Gold). The shadowing forth of Our Lord Lucifer, as the Powers of Darkness gather at a midnight mass. The dance of the Magus widdershins around the Swirling Spiral Force, the solar swastika, until the Bringer of Light – Lucifer –

breaks through.

"The true Magick of Horus requires the passionate union of opposites."

–Aleister Crowley

LUCIFER RISING (1970–81)

30 min. Color. Sound (Music by Bobby Beausoleil and the Freedom Orchestra, Tracy Prison). Filmed in Luxor, Karnak, Gizeh, London, Exernsteine, Avebury.

Credits: Conceived, Directed, Photographed, and Edited by Kenneth Anger. Assistant Camera: Michael Cooper. Thelemic consultant: Gerald J Yorke. A presentation of Anita Pallenberg. Cast: Miriam Gibril (Isis); Donald Cammell (Osiris); Haydn Couts (Adept); Kenneth Anger (Magus); Sir Francis Rose (Chaos); Marianne Faithfull (Lilith); Leslie Huggins (Lucifer). Anger edited a 25-minute version of *Lucifer Rising* in 1973, featuring a soundtrack by Jimmy Page of Led Zeppelin. In 1976 he removed Page from the film and prepared the final edit (with additional footage and optical effects) which Bobby Beausoleil scored from prison. Although originally conceived as the first part of a larger, serial work, this version of Lucifer now stands as a completed film in its own right.

Lucifer Rising was Anger's last released film for the next twenty years. He meanwhile applied his craft to re-working details of the *Magick Lantern Cycle*, pruning and tightening or adding extra material, such as new soundtracks. The only new projects mentioned in the 70s were two "limited edition" reels, of which only scant details appeared from Abby Hirsch

Publications of New York. These were:

SENATORS IN BONDAGE (1976)

Color, sound, 16mm; price $1,776.

"The Eisenstein of Satanism strikes again! Prints of Kenneth Anger's first limited edition, *Senators In Bondage* – edition strictly limited to 13 copies in honour of the original 13 colonies. The master negative will be sealed; no further prints will be struck. Each print individually hand-colored, supplied in a red, white and blue box, bound in chain. *Senators In Bondage* – a movie metaphor of mighty eminences brought low. A vitriolic bon-bon concocted with malice; a curio for this bicentennial year."

MATELOTS EN MENOTTES (1977)

Color, sound, 16mm; price $1,200.

"*Matelots En Menottes* – a return to the original subject of *Fireworks*. Kenneth Anger's second limited edition. Edition strictly limited to 12 copies."

Anger would later comment: "[the limited edition films] grew out of a group of people that I knew in Paris who were collectors of limited edition books, largely erotica. ... And so I suggested that wouldn't it be amusing to make the same idea of a limited edition book as a film, and have it just for ten copies or something. So I made it a private experiment. I never intended to sell enough of them to make any real money. But at least I got these little films made, and they were erotic – but not pornographic. Maybe one day they will surface. ... There were four shorts. They were just like ten minutes each and I sold them to four or five different people, mostly in France."

In 1987, a new film, *Mouse Heaven*, was announced, but soon abandoned, only to resurface some 16 years later. It would not be until the end of the millennium that Anger began work in earnest on a new project, which went under the working title of *A Hitler Youth's Dream*. In the early years of the 21st century Anger completed several short video works; these include *Don't Smoke That Cigarette* (2000), *Anger Sees Red* (2004), *Elliott's Suicide* (2007), *I'll Be Watching You* (2007), *Foreplay* (2008), and *My Surfing Lucifer* (2009). The three most interesting examples of this new output were:

THE MAN WE WANT TO HANG (2002)

Anger was one of the mainstays of an exhibition of Aleister Crowley's paintings at the October Gallery in Bloomsbury, London, in 1998, where he gave a slide presentation on his experiences at Thelema Abbey. *The Man We Want To Hang* documents the exhibition, with detailed close-ups of Crowley's vivid images. With a score by Liadov. This exploration of Crowley's art was continued by Anger in *Brush Of Baphomet* (2009).

MOUSE HEAVEN (2004)

Conceived in 1987, on hold for the next 16 years, *Mouse Heaven* is a fantastical collage of Mickey Mouse toys and imagery, incorporating animated models, prints and original footage.

ICH WILL! (2008)

A brilliant 35-minute montage of Nazi glory, focusing on the Hitler Youth movement and their fanatical devotions, using rare 1930s archive material – propaganda footage, home movies and newsreel – rousingly scored and deftly assembled. Scenes of bonding, discipline amd calisthenics soon give way to images of force and fire, Nazi rallies and rites ignited and illuminated by blazing swastikas.

4. MISCELLANEA

THE DEAD (1960)

Directed by Stan Brakhage, 11 minutes, silent.

Filmed in Père Lachaise Cemetery, along the Seine, and in a café, where Anger appears.

LOOK BACK AT ANGER (1974)

Directed by Leo Vale, 12 minutes.

A film portrait featuring Anger discussing his work, intercut with extracts and old movie stills.

NIGHT OF PAN (2009)

Directed by Brian Butler, 8 minutes.

Anger, Vincent Gallo, and director Butler conduct an occult ritual that symbolizes the stage of ego death in the process of spiritual attainment.

NOTES

1. It is possible that Anger burned all his films made before *Fireworks* in October 1967, as part of his reaction to the theft of the original footage of *Lucifer Rising*.

2. Anger claims to have been making and screening films since the age of 7, when he filmed a version of *Ferdinand The Bull*: "...In *Ferdinand* I had the bull (two boys under a skin) played effeminate..."

–Tony Rayns, *Anger Kompendium*

3. Beausoleil derived the nickname "Cupid" from a character he played in the 1966 movie *Mondo Hollywood*. His other movie roles included a part in the porno Western *Ramrodder* (1967).

4. Anger himself has described the "epitaph" episode as a "public exorcism" of his outrage and grief at losing *Lucifer Rising* (quoted in Rebekah Wood, "Flames In The Night").

5. In *The Family* (1971), Ed Sanders reports Anger's presence in Washington as follows: "While various Diggers and exorcists were standing atop the flat-bed truck screeching 'Out Demons Out', Anger, bare from the waist up, revealing what appeared to be a tattoo of Lucifer upon his chest, burned a picture of the Devil within a consecrated pentagram, shouting oaths and hissing as he flashed a magic ring at inquiring reporters thrusting microphones at him hunched down in the gravel" (p.43).

6. For a while, Anger had hopes that Mick Jagger would be his new *Lucifer*.

"...The Magus instructed Jagger as to what rare occult books to purchase at London's more exclusive antiquaries. It was during the time that Anger served as the Rolling Stones' court wizard that Jagger read the 1930s novel *The Master And Margherita* by Mikhail Bulgakov, which tells the tale of Satan's visit to Russia after the revolution. The novel, and Anger's positive conception of Lucifer, inspired Jagger to write that enduring infernal anthem `Sympathy For The Devil'..."

–Nikolas Schreck, *The Satanic Screen,* p.132.

TABLE OF ILLUSTRATIONS

COLOUR SECTION